The Life and Death of Almost Everybody

A Play

David Campton

A SAMUEL FRENCH ACTING EDITION

SAMUEL
FRENCH
FOUNDED 1830

SAMUELFRENCH-LONDON.CO.UK
SAMUELFRENCH.COM

FOR AMATEUR PRODUCTION ENQUIRIES

UNITED KINGDOM AND WORLD
EXCLUDING NORTH AMERICA
plays@SamuelFrench-London.co.uk
020 7255 4302/01

Each title is subject to availability from Samuel French,

depending upon country of performance.

Opening monologue.

CAST

Sweeper - employed to sweep theatre stage

Young Man

Young Woman

Aunt Harriet

Mr Broom

Mrs Broom

Mr Guide

Mrs Guide

Indignant Person

Emissary

Messenger

Voice in Crowd—Heckler

Girl

Court Official

1st Guard

2nd Guard

Chief of Police

Manager

Brooms, Guides, Heralds, Soldiers, Crowd

(Deadly Sins—Lust, Envy, Avarice, Gluttony, Anger, Sloth)

The section of the second act between asterisks * * * may, if desired, be omitted in production. This would remove the Deadly Sins

The Life and Death of Almost Everybody was presented at the Questors, Ealing (England), as part of their new play festival in June, 1970. The director was Bill McLaughlin

ACT I

An empty stage

The house Lights are on in the auditorium with a working light over the stage

A man with a brush appears and starts to sweep the stage. After a while he pauses

Sweeper Dust. Dust. Every particle guaranteed to last. If the world went bang, and blew us all across the universe, there'd still be dust—drifting across the light years to settle on some other planet: piling up in corners, waiting for a brush. Listen to it. Just listen. Patter-patter. Where I've just cleaned. Turn your back, and it's landed again. Leave it a year, and it's piled up an inch thick. Come again in a thousand years and you'll find it knee-deep. You don't believe me? Come back in a thousand years and check. What's that? In a thousand years we'll all be dust? Let's have a grand reunion then. Let's have fun with some other poor twit. Patter-patter. Where he's just been with his brush. "Don't worry, chum," we'll tell him. "Join the party." Mind you, I'm not claiming that's an original thought. I never have original thoughts now. A long time ago I thought that I might: then I discovered they'd all been thought before. They seem to float in the air. Like dust. (*He sweeps in silence for a few strokes*) I'm paid for this. My duties were carefully detailed when I was taken on. All the musts and must nots. Keep the stage clean, I was told. Actors have to fall down on that stage. They roll round when they fight, die, make love. Sometimes even in the plays. A dirty floor distresses the wardrobe mistress. Well, if you've nothing better to do, you can watch me. See? That's how it's done. Nice, easy movements. Professional. If you want to learn how to use a brush, I know my job backwards. (*He sweeps*) This is the way I like a stage. Bare. Anything can happen on a bare stage. Whenever I see a bare stage I get an itch. I want to . . . Beg pardon. I was somewhat transported. Besides, The Manager said I mustn't. (*He sweeps*) You leave the stage alone, The Manager warned me. Clean it, yes. Leave it as spotless as a Guardsman's badge; but that's the limit of your involvement. You regard the stage as sacred, he instructed me. With an empty stage you can be tempted to play God, and that's a high-voltage game. You don't want to get yourself blasted, do you? He dissuaded me. A stage can be a source of danger. Sweep it, yes. Scrub it, yes. Dust out the corners if the mood moves you. But, for pity's sake, don't go tampering with it. A stage has to be approached in the proper frame of mind, The Manager advised me. It's a key-hole for peering into the unknown. But don't you go opening any doors, he cautioned me. You might let something out you can't push back. You're a good man with a brush, he flattered me. You stick to your brush. A brush is safe. Not like a stage. You leave that stage alone, or else, he threatened me. Don't you go playing God, he shouted at me. (*He sweeps*) So I didn't. (*He sweeps*) Not much. Only a bit when everybody was out, and the doors were locked, and no more than this working light to see by. (*He sweeps*) I made up a jungle once. Not much of a jungle really—no more than from here to there. But it had long grass as high as a man, and clawing bushes, and strangulating vines, and trees that shut out the light. The usual jungle. No animals, though. I wasn't up to animals at that stage. Just noises. Cheeps in the high branches, and twitterings in the bushes, and swish, swish, swish in the long grass. Slow and sinuous and heavy and slithering in the long grass. Swish, swish, swish. Nearer, and nearer, and nearer. Swish. So I gave up the jungle, and went on to a ballroom. (*He dances with his brush*) One-two-three. One-two-three. One-two-three. You look ravishing tonight, Your Highness. When may one ravish? But there was no audience, then. It's the audience that constitutes the danger. It's the audience that builds up the voltage. When you start to create something, it's the audience that won't let you drop it. Nobody told me that: I worked it out for myself. I can watch, can't I? I can see what goes on. It's the audience. I never had an audience before. I never . . . But The Manager said I mustn't. (*He sweeps*) But a tiny idea couldn't matter so much. Not as long as I made it quite clear who's in control. A rabbit now . . . (*He puts down his brush and crouches, looking at something a few feet in front of him. He beckons to it*) Come on now. Come on, Bunny. You're not afraid, are you? Of course not. I won't hurt you. You know that. Come on, then. Come on, boy. Jump. (*He catches the imaginary rabbit in his arms, and stands up, cradling it*) There. A rabbit. Long ears, white tail, and all. Trembling a bit. He's not used to humans—even imaginary humans. Better let him go again. (*He puts the "rabbit" down, and claps his hands*) Off you go. Don't let the butcher get you. Did you see it? You're not using your imagination. I can't do all the work. It might help if the lights were different—if it was lighter here, where I am, and darker where you are. It's not essential, but I am only a beginner. So try to imagine it's darker there, and lighter here. Imagine. Please. Imagine. (*The house Lights fade out. A pool of Light over the Sweeper* c *comes up. The working Light goes out*) That's better. That's what imagination can do for you. Now something really big. A man and a woman. I never tried with a man and a woman before. That's really taking a chance. Men and women have minds of their own. The Manager told me so. That's what makes them different. That's what makes them dangerous. Well, I shan't give them minds, so there's nothing to be afraid of. They'll just do as they're told. And if they don't do as they're told, I can always unthink them—like the rabbit. Steady now. This is the most fantastic trick I ever pulled. You don't believe I can do it, do you? Well, don't think about me. Think about them. A man and A Woman.

A Young Man and Young Woman emerge from the shadows at the back of the stage. They are dressed in a neutral costume. Their faces are expressionless. Their bodies are quite relaxed, but equally expressionless. They walk into the light, and stand waiting—two mindless bodies

That's some creation, that is. Personally I half-expected a round of applause. But perhaps you're right. They need work. This is only a rough sketch. The refinements come later.

He picks up one of the Young Woman's arms, then lets it go. It flops to her side. He pushes the Young Man forward: the Young Man returns to an upright position

I had hoped for something more spectacular myself. Not necessarily the Black and White Minstrel Show. But at least some sign of life. (*Shouting*) You're alive! You and you! Alive!

Young Man I'm alive.

Young Woman I'm alive.

Sweeper Isn't that worth throwing your hat into the air for? Isn't that worth writing to *The Times* about? You're alive. Being alive opens a multitude of possibilities. Try some of them.

Young Woman We cannot.

Young Man We have no minds of our own.

Sweeper You're not having any, either. I follow the instructions on the packet. I keep the bottle corked and out of the reach of children. I light the blue paper and retire immediately.

Young Man No minds.

Young Woman No minds of our own.

Sweeper You're a man and you're a woman. I arranged matters that way. Doesn't that make a difference?

Young Man I am a man?

Young Woman I am a woman?

Sweeper Look at each other. Enjoy yourselves.

Young Man Hello, Woman.

Young Woman Hello, Man.

Sweeper There's enthusiasm for you. I went to a lot of trouble to imagine you two. Appreciate it. Get to know each other.

Young Man I have an articulated core with a spongy outer layer protected by a decorative covering. I am equipped with instruments for perceiving sound, light, taste, smell, and texture I have an internal combustion system, and a genito-urinary apparatus.

Sweeper Well, what do you know?

Young Man We know.

Young Woman We have minds. But not minds of our own.

Sweeper Well, don't just stand there. Function.

The Young Man does a knee bend. He stands up. As he does so the Young Woman does a knee bend. They bend and stretch alternately

I've seen better entertainment in a goldfish bowl. At least give it vocal accompaniment.

Young Man Up.
Young Woman Down.
Young Man Up.
Young Woman Down.
Young Man Up.
Young Woman Down.
Sweeper Stop!

They stop

You're tempting me, that's what you're doing. Well, it won't work. You're not getting me to break the rules. You're not getting me to dive off the deep end. You're not getting me to push the button. But honestly the rabbit was more fun.
Young Man You imagined the rabbit.
Sweeper Yes, I imagined the rabbit. Then I rubbed it out.
Young Man You imagined us.
Young Woman You can rub us out.
Young Man You can go forwards.
Young Woman You can go backwards.
Young Man Or you can stay as you are.
Young Woman You can give us minds of our own.
Young Man You can rub us out.
Young Woman Or you can leave us as we are.
Young Man Forwards.
Young Woman Backwards.
Young Man Stop.
Young Woman Forwards.
Young Man Backwards.
Young Woman Stop.
Young Man Forwards.
Young Woman Backwards.
Sweeper Stop! Don't you tell me what to do. I'm in charge of this opera-tion. (*He picks up his brush, and leans on it pensively*) Yes, I'm in charge. (*To the Audience*) I can always scrap the experiment. Any time I choose. It's not as if they were real. They don't exist apart from me. You can only see them because I'm thinking about them. And if I forget them, they'll go back into thin air. So what's the worry? Anyway, they're no use as they are—except perhaps to C and A's. I don't want to do away with them. They're attractive in a messy sort of way. I made them. So what now?... You know what I'm going to do as well as I do. Am I reading your thoughts, or are you reading mine? (*He tosses the brush away*) All right, you two. From now on you're on your own.

The Young Man and Young Woman look at each other. They take deep breaths. The Young Man strolls casually in a circle round the Young Woman, eyeing her surreptitiously. The Young Woman pretends to be in-volved with something else, but keeps him in view out of the corner of her eye. The Sweeper continues to address them while this is going on

Within reason, naturally. I'm still the chap who tells you what to do. But you can please yourself how you do it—as long as it's done promptly, cheerfully, and efficiently, without offending the Watch Committee. That's called Free Will.

The Young Man comes to rest by the side of the Young Woman. They glance at each other

This bit is called "Boy Meets Girl". It has to come sooner or later, so let's get it over with. "But soft, what light through yonder window breaks." Take it from there.

Young Man Seen you around, haven't I?

Young Woman I've been around.

Young Woman Thought I'd seen you around.

Young Woman I've seen you, too. Around.

Young Man I've been around.

Young Woman That's where I've seen you. Around.

Young Man Yes. You might say I'd been around.

Young Woman Thought I'd seen you around.

Sweeper For that they need minds?

Young Woman Then I'll be seeing you around.

Sweeper No.

Young Man No?

Young Woman Did you say no?

Young Man No.

Young Woman Somebody said no.

Sweeper You've got feelings, passions . . .

Young Man I've got feelings, passions . . .

Young Woman I can feel your passions.

Sweeper Hot blood.

Young Man My blood . . .

Young Woman It's hot.

Sweeper You mean something to each other.

Young Man We mean . . . (*He turns to look at the Sweeper*) There are some strange characters in these parts.

Young Woman They listen to conversations.

Young Man Private conversations . . . Hey, you. Strange character.

Young Woman We're having a private conversation.

Young Man A private conversation is impossible when strange characters are listening.

Young Woman So please leave us alone, strange character.

Young Man Depart.

Sweeper Do you know who I am?

Young Man It's a game.

Young Woman Do you mind if we don't join in? We'd rather have a private conversation . . . Coming?

Sweeper You listen to me.

Young Woman Sorry . . . Coming?

Sweeper You can't leave me.

Young Woman We do have minds of our own. Coming?

Sweeper Because I invented you. That's why. I made you up.

Young Woman You made us up?

Sweeper Out of my own head.

The Young Man and Young Woman look at each other

Young Woman Of course, that explains everything.

Young Man If only you'd said earlier.

Young Woman I've often wondered where I came from. This disposes of the whole question.

Young Man He made us up.

Young Woman Out of his own head. I had been told of other ways.

Young Man Storks.

Young Woman Gooseberry bushes.

Young Man Little black bags.

Sweeper You're laughing at me.

Young Woman Oh, no. We're agreeing with you.

Young Man I was always told—if you meet a strange character who says he's just made you up out of his own head: for God's sake agree with him.

Sweeper This is what it means to be an artist. Your own creation turns round and calls you a nut case.

Young Woman My mother always said . . .

Sweeper Your mother?

Young Woman I had a mother.

Sweeper Go on.

Young Woman My mother said . . . (*She frowns as she tries to remember what her mother said*) She said . . . (*To the Young Man*) What did your mother say?

Young Man You leave my mother out of this.

Sweeper What's her name?

Young Woman Mother.

Sweeper What's his name?

Young Woman How should I know?

Sweeper What's *your* name?

Young Woman You're asking a lot of questions.

Young Man You leave her alone.

Sweeper You, then. What's your name? Where do you live? When did you last see your father?

The Young Man tries to think, but meets with a blank

Young Man You've got no right. Where's your authority? You've got no right.

Sweeper Where are you going when you leave here?

Young Man You tell us, if you're so clever.

Sweeper Not to that tone of voice. You learn respect.

Young Man At least we know where we are.

Sweeper Do you?

Young Man We're here. So you can go and chase yourself, chum—if you care for that sort of sport.
Sweeper Where's here?
Young Man Next to her.
Young Woman Next to him.
Sweeper Hyde Park Corner? Empire State Building? Red Square?

The Young Man puts his arm around the Young Woman. She puts her arms around him

Young Woman We'll stay here. Wherever it is.
Sweeper You're stuck. You may have minds of your own, but you depend on me. You depend on me to tell you who you are, and what you are, and where you are. You're stuck until I give you the next move.
Young Woman Goody-goody.

She and the Young Man kiss

Sweeper Sooner or later the kissing has to stop.
Young Man Why?

They kiss

Sweeper You can't keep that up for ever.
Young Woman We can try.

They kiss

Sweeper All right. Here's a new trick. An hour later.

The Young Man and Young Woman part, panting. Then kiss again

Five hours later.

The Young Man and Young Woman, still kissing, sink to their knees

Next day.

The Young Man and Young Woman, exhausted, sink to the floor but still in each other's arms

Very interesting—as an endurance test. This could develop into a difficult situation. Never lose control of your creations—that's a prime rule. Look at Henry One Vee Parts One and Two. A funny old fat man comes on to play a bit part, and walks off with the play. Kings and Queens, Lords and Ladies, all kept waiting while he does his drunk act. The only way to get him off the stage in time for Henry Vee was to kill him. But I don't want to kill these off just yet. I want to explore their potential. When *they* stop exploring. (*Heavily*) They wake, and consider their future.

The Young Man and Young Woman sit up

Young Man I think we ought to get married.
Young Woman I think you're right.

Young Man Don't mind me asking this . . . I mean—we'd have got round to it sooner or later. After all, we're mature people. Not that it really matters, but . . . What *is* your name?

Young Woman (*in a temporary panic*) Elsie Drinkwater.

Sweeper That's a lie for a start.

Young Man Are you still here?

Young Woman Iris Gloucestershire. Something like that.

Sweeper Nothing like that. Got you now. You'll never get any minister to say "Will you—um—take this woman—er—to be your lawful wedded." You can't even carry her over the threshold until I tell you where the threshold is.

Young Man I can. It's—it's—it's—it's just on the tip of my tongue.

Young Woman It—just slipped my . . . Marcia Imskip?

Sweeper No.

Young Woman Brenda Gladstone?

Sweeper No.

Young Man You stole our minds. What do you want?

Sweeper I want you to realize who's responsible for you, that's what.

Young Woman Great bully.

Young Man (*now desperately*) I can't think. I can't think.

Young Woman There, there. What does a silly old name matter? I'm here. You'd sooner have me without a name than a name without me, wouldn't you? Anna May Wong.

Sweeper Before your time.

Young Woman All right. Help us.

Sweeper What a way to ask.

Young Woman Please, then.

Young Man Help us. Please.

Sweeper Who made you?

Young Woman How should we know?

Sweeper Who—made—you?

Young Man You did.

Sweeper That's better.

Young Woman Out of your own head you made us.

Young Man We are your creations.

Sweeper Now we know where we are. It was a near go, but I brought 'em into line. We're having no little Falstaffs in this theatre.

Young Woman Please.

Sweeper Eve. I know it's symbolic; but a symbol or two keeps the critics happy. Gives them something to get their teeth into. Keep chewing, lads. I'll toss in more later.

Young Woman I'm Eve. I've always been Eve.

Young Man Adam?

Sweeper Go ahead.

Young Man Sure. I remember now. I live . . .

Sweeper New estate.

Young Man Big block.

Sweeper Top flat.

Young Man Panoramic view. All those lovely factory chimneys. Acres of roof tops. Shunting yards and the gas works. It's all there. I live with . . .

Sweeper The family.

Young Man Dad's . . .

Sweeper Shop steward. Boilermaker's Union. I just invented him.

Young Man Come off it. He's fifty if he's a day. And what about my grand-dad? Over seventy. Don't tell me you were around when *he* came into the world.

Sweeper You're beginning to disbelieve. You're slipping again already.

Young Woman Don't slip yet, love. He stopped at my name.

Young Man You created her, did you? I reckon you did a good job there.

Young Woman }
Sweeper } Thank you. }*(Speaking together)*

Young Man Your own unaided work?

Sweeper Helped out by memories and a few reliable works of reference. *Penthouse*, you know, for the basic structural details. *King. Playmate of the Month* with the creases ironed out.

Young Man Perhaps you'd better fill me in on her mother.

Sweeper A pillar of the Townswomen's Guild.

Young Woman Oh, definitely. Jam and chutney all over the place. And they rehearse little plays in our lounge.

Sweeper Through lounge, semi-detached, with garage space.

Young Woman I suppose I've been lucky with my parents. When I leave home to get married, I shan't miss either of them.

Sweeper Married?

Young Woman Surely you haven't forgotten. This is one wedding I'm not missing.

Sweeper All right then. Six months later.

Young Woman Already? Excuse me. A little woman round the corner. Satin and lace. Shan't be a minute.

The Young Woman runs off into the darkness

Sweeper (*to the Young Man*) Aren't you getting ready, too? Try Moss Bros. The bride's father insists. Pictures in the local press. Can't have him in morning suit, and you in jeans.

Young Man This last six months went by like a flash. A few back seats at the pictures. A couple of walks. Wham!

Sweeper I'm just going to announce the guests.

Young Man I say . . .

Sweeper She's waiting at the church.

Young Man White collars and boiler suits. I mean—you've worked out the next episode, have you?

Sweeper I'm playing this by ear.

Young Man It may be as good as a play to you, but it's our lives that are being played around with. Just watch your step.

Sweeper Me?

Young Man See you at the church.

The Young Man walks jauntily off into the darkness

Sweeper If I don't watch out, they'll be telling me what to do. This would be a good place to pack up and go home. They wouldn't be any worse off. They'd just cease to exist. Quite painlessly. Just slipping from one darkness to another—no more than going off under an anaesthetic. After all, we haven't known them long enough to become really fond of them. Anyway, it was struggle enough to keep *them* in order, without having to face up to his father. Or her mother. Or what happened when . . . (*Pause*) Oh, what's the use! You can't just say "Once upon a time . . ." and then stop. The Reception. Cake, canapes, champagne, and another hundred on Daddy's overdraft.

The Lights come up to full. There is the sound of distant music and a gabble of guests

On my right—the Brooms.

As the Sweeper announces, the Young Man's family enter R. *Mrs Broom wears on her head an extravagant pile of flowers, ribbon and muslin. She peers about her like a bewildered tourist in an overstocked palace. Mr Broom bears himself with cautious importance*

(*Announcing*) Mr Broom, Mrs Broom, and various other Brooms. (*Confidentially*) They're a bit exaggerated, but whose family isn't?

Broom As I remarked to the *maitre d'hôtel*, the champagne is adequate. Very adequate. Hold your head up, Mother: we're under observation.

Mrs Broom I was looking at the carpet. Just like our Liz's. She said at the time it was genuine Persian. Out of the market. I'm glad I didn't believe her.

Broom You're a disappointment, Mother.

Mrs Broom I know, Arthur. But not here. Not now.

Broom Look them in the eye. Allow the opposition to establish a position of superiority, and you are jackbooted into the mire.

Mrs Broom Later, Arthur. You can lecture me in bed tonight, but this is his wedding.

Broom Where's the lad's ambition?

Mrs Broom She'll push him on. She's got the eyes and chin for it.

Broom Join the management? Isn't he cognisant that there is no lower animal than the perpetual junior executive? Hasn't he scrutinized her father?

Mrs Broom Here they come, Arthur. Be nice to them. Don't call them Fascist hyenas this afternoon.

Sweeper (*announcing*) Mr Guide. Mrs Guide. An assortment of Guides.

The Young Woman's family enter from the L. *Mr Guide is fretful and nervous. For Mrs Guide the occasion is a pill with insufficient sugar*

Mrs Guide Smile, darling. Smile.
Guide They're swilling the champagne like soda water.
Mrs Guide I know it hurts, but smile. The side smiling the longest is the
winner. Smile at the father, darling. That speech! The first time I've sat
through *Das Kapital* at a wedding. Your jokes were painful enough,
but at least we knew when to laugh. Smile at mother. That hat! Not
even Royalty could get away with it. You gave the bride away, darling.
Smile as though you meant it.
Sweeper All a bit stereotyped, but what do you expect at short notice . . .?
Here comes the happy couple. (*He leads the applause*)

The Young Man and Young Woman enter, wearing nuptial accessories.
The couple stop on seeing the Sweeper

Young Man Don't look now.
Sweeper There's a welcome.
Young Woman You're not exactly what a radiant bride expects.
Young Man We hoped you'd given up. You haven't been seen for weeks.
Sweeper I've been here all the time.
Young Woman That explains it. *There* isn't here.
Sweeper You can't do anything without me being around.
Young Woman That's a fine thing to say at a wedding.
Young Man Anyway, you weren't with the lads last night.
Young Woman Or at Maison Veronique. She wouldn't have stood for an
eye at her fitting-room keyhole.
Sweeper There wasn't a booze-up last night. Or a fitting with Madame
Veronica. I skipped all that.
Young Man You might, but we didn't.
Young Woman I don't know where you skip to, but we live each moment
as it comes. Every scotch. Every stitch. Something tells me you don't
know everything.
Sweeper Something tells me I'm learning.
Young Woman This is very disillusioning. I'm not sure I believe in you as
much as I did.
Sweeper You'd better. That's all I can say.
Young Man It isn't saying very much. But if you don't mind . . .
Young Woman The guests.
Young Man After all . . .
Young Woman It is our wedding.
Young Man Enjoy yourself. It's on the house.

The Young Man joins the Guides. The Young Woman goes to the Brooms.
There is laughter and chatter from each group

Sweeper One character is easy. Two take watching. But you can't keep
your eye on a couple of dozen all at once.

The guests circulate. The movement has a suggestion of a country dance
"chain" about it

A Broom Such a nice girl.

A Broom Such a pity.

A Guide What a pleasant boy.

A Guide What a waste.

A Broom They met by accident.

A Guide A disaster.

A Broom Such a pity.

A Guide Such a waste.

A Broom Prospects.

A Guide Prospects.

A Broom Any number.

A Guide Turned down.

A Broom No background.

A Guide None at all.

A Broom Such a nice boy.

A Guide Such a pleasant girl.

A Broom
A Guide } Such a happy couple } (*Speaking together*)

Sweeper What did I let loose?

He is joined by a sharp female of indeterminate age—Harriet

Harriet I am the Aunt Harriet.

Sweeper The who?

Harriet *The* Aunt Harriet. Should I know you?

Sweeper I don't know you.

Harriet That is immaterial.

Sweeper I mean—I never said "There's an Aunt Harriet".

Harriet There's always an Aunt Harriet. Weddings and funerals. Always there. Are you one of the Brooms? Such a pleasant boy.

Sweeper No, I'm ...

Harriet A Guide. Such a nice girl.

Sweeper I'm trying to remember where ...

Harriet An irrelevance. As long as I remember you. That *is* important. Five—ten—twenty years on, when the cake has all crumbled, and they can't remember where they put the photographs—"Do you remember that strange man," I'll say. "The one who stood in a corner, muttering to himself." And they'll remember you. You're not a Guide either, are you? I thought not. Press?

Sweeper I've seen you before.

Harriet Between ourselves, I arranged everything. I never boast, but I know where the credit lies. Look at his family: look at hers. How did it happen? Aunt Harriet. *The* Aunt Harriet.

Sweeper Now I remember. Not all of a piece, but ... We had a neighbour.

Harriet Ada Figginbotham.

Sweeper Running round with a scrap of scandal, like a chicken with a bit of straw. She knew everything. Like my schoolteacher. Oh, that one was a tough nut. Bony fingers digging into the piano keys ...

Harriet One-two. One-two. One-two.

Sweeper Old Gimlet-eyes. One suck of a peardrop at the back of the desk, and she'd got you. Hard, yes. My sister had a wooden doll like her—a Dutch doll. Name of Harriet.

Harriet So you're that boy, are you? Grubby beast with a running nose.

Sweeper But I didn't invent you. '

Harriet Knocked out his sister's front tooth and was caught writing on the wall.

Sweeper You're one of those bit-part menaces. You slipped in with the extras; now you're trying to steal a scene. Get back into the crowd.

Harriet Once an Aunt Harriet, always an Aunt Harriet. (*She rejoins a group, and disappears within it*)

Sweeper And you lot—get on with the reception.

The two groups suddenly separate, leaving Mrs Guide glaring at Mr Broom

Mrs Guide That remark was uncalled for. Apologize.

Young Woman Mother!

Broom Beg pardon of a statistical irrelevance?

Young Man Dad!

Guide You are talking to my wife, sir. Less of your shop-floor jargon.

Mrs Broom Arthur never spoke jargon in his life: did you, Arthur?

Broom Mother, the time has come to effect a departure.

Young Man No, you don't.

Broom To descend to the vernacular, lad—we've seen you spliced, now they can get knotted.

Young Man I'm not having my wedding broken up by politics.

Mrs Broom It wasn't politics: it was millinery.

Young Woman You need never meet again, but let's have a civilized wedding.

Young Man Grit your teeth and be friends.

Mrs Broom There's nothing wrong with my hat.

Young Man Just for this afternoon.

Guide Whose collar would look ridiculous on a horse?

Young Woman Please.

Broom There's only one reply to managerial intransigence—withdrawal of labour.

Young Woman No!

Guide Let them go while the champagne lasts.

Young Woman If they go now, the feud will last for ever.

Broom Come, Brooms. Avail yourselves of public transport.

Young Man You there.

Sweeper Me?

Young Woman Stop them. Do something.

Young Man Anything.

Sweeper Stop!

The Brooms stop on their way to the exit. Mr Broom turns and looks at the Sweeper

Broom Are you making a proposal, brother?

Sweeper I said "stop".

Broom We agreed to vacate these premises. It was a decision arrived at by democratic procedures.

Sweeper Scrap it.

Broom Not even for a brother, brother.

The Brooms head for the exit again

Young Woman Can't you stop them?

Sweeper Of course I can. Come back!

The Brooms back several paces

Broom Well?

Sweeper Stay where you are.

Broom It's a free country.

The Brooms go out

Young Man You can't do it.

Young Woman I knew we were fools to believe in you.

Sweeper (*desperately*) They can't leave. The lift's broken down, and this is the thirteenth floor, and there'll be twenty-six flights of stairs to go down to reach the street.

Mrs Guide So high? I could have sworn we started the party on the ground floor.

Sweeper I did it.

Young Man Did what?

Sweeper Oh-ho, you soon pick up the knack of running the world. Human beings think they can get away with murder, but they're at the mercy of things. Control things: control the world.

The Brooms return, grumbling

Broom Typical, decadent, capitalist machinery.

Mrs Broom We haven't changed our minds. But I couldn't hobble all that way in these heels.

Broom The lift has ceased to function.

Mrs Broom It won't work.

Sweeper How's that, you unbelievers?

Young Woman You knew all the time the lift was broken.

Young Man That wasn't so clever.

Sweeper Oh, you ungrateful pair.

Broom I'd be obliged if you would inform the management of our predicament.

Mrs Guide Delighted—if you'll fetch him from his office. It's on the ground floor.

Mrs Broom We'll just have to stay drinking till relief comes.

Guide The champagne! This is the hotel's fault. I'll dispute the bill.

Young Woman If you're not a fraud, give us something to believe in. Give us peace.

Sweeper Right. But I want something in return.

Young Man Such as?

Sweeper Respect.

Young Woman You get that when you've earned it.

Sweeper Co-operation.

Mrs Broom I'm worried about the kiddies when they come—poor little things.

Young Man It's a bargain.

Young Woman If it works.

Sweeper You watch. (*As though telling a story*) "Suddenly Mr Broom throws back his head and laughs."

Broom does so, to the consternation of the rest of the group

Young Man Where does that get us?

Sweeper "Come, friends," he cries.

Broom makes a great embracing gesture

"Let us dispose of this needless quarrel."

As the Sweeper recounts the action, the Brooms and Guides mime it with extravagant gestures

Young Man It's not the way you say it, so much as what is said. That doesn't sound like my dad.

Sweeper Who's telling this story?

Young Man Over to you.

Sweeper With outstretched hands Mr Broom crosses to Mr Guide. For a moment Mr Guide holds back, suspicious of this sudden token of friendship. But Mr Broom persists, still smiling, still offering the hand of reconciliation. Suddenly Mr Guide's reserve cracks. He thrusts aside his old animosity, and the two men shake hands. They embrace and pat each other on the back.

Young Woman It's working. I don't know how he does it, but it's working.

Sweeper Then they think of their wives—still standing cold and aloof. Can this new joy be brought to their womenfolk? Can they likewise be brought into the fold?

Young Man Don't miss next week's thrilling instalment.

Young Woman Take no notice of him. You'll never win the Nobel Prize for Literature, but you're doing all right.

Sweeper The two men appeal to their wives. "Come, wife. Join this happy reunion." Taking their ladies by the arm, they bring them face to face. "Let the sun not go down on your wrath," they plead. The women are overcome. They weep, embrace, kiss each other, and weep again. Even the menfolk secretly wipe the tears from their eyes. Joy reigns.

Young Man But what about the others?

Sweeper Oh, yes. Fellowship is infectious. The two groups slap each other on the back, choked with emotion. They join hands, singing "For They Are Jolly Good Fellows".

From behind the group a piercing voice is heard

Harriet Drunk, of course. (*She emerges*) All drunk.

Sweeper You again?

Harriet That conversion won't outlast the hangover. Thick-headed, bleary-eyed, with queasy insides, the two groups draw apart again. "Cheap champagne," moans one lot. "The amount they swilled," groans the other.

Young Man It's my Aunt Harriet.

Young Woman I thought she was my aunt.

Harriet I'm everybody's aunt.

Sweeper I'm not having you mucking up my peace-keeping operations.

Harriet Look at them next morning—groping for the bicarb, the hot water, the Alka-Seltzer. Watch them trying to work out where they put their teeth, wondering how their socks came to be in the fridge. And what happens when they recall their late brotherly love? Horror!

The group expresses all this

Sweeper You have no right to be here. These people exist in my mind.

Harriet So do I. You remembered me yourself. If you don't like me, blame your nasty nature.

Young Woman Are you going to let her break up the party?

Young Man Peace. That's all we want.

Sweeper That's what you're going to have.

Harriet Sweetness and light? Either you're cheating, or you don't know much about the human race. War is its natural condition. Give men more than five minutes' peace, and they'll dream up outlets for their aggressions. Deny them a common enemy, and they'll turn on themselves.

Sweeper Not here. I'll outlaw all weapons.

Harriet They've tongues like swords, dear boy.

The groups mutter among themselves. Odd sentences are heard, and these become faster and faster

A Broom I'm open-minded, but on the doorstep in broad daylight . . .

A Guide Heathenish, no matter how you look at it.

Broom It's their religion, you know. They go straight to Heaven after.

Guide Drummed into them from childhood. After that you can't get it out.

Broom It's not them: it's their cooking.

Guide When a dog's a nuisance, you put it down.

Broom I don't wish them any harm, but if it's for the good of everyone.

Guide It would be a kindness. You wouldn't want them to suffer.

Broom It's in the blood.

Guide Yes, it's in the blood

Broom Blood.

Guide Blood.

Brooms and Guides Blood!

The voices are stopped by a laugh from Harriet

Harriet There's the fuse. Anyone have a match?
Young Woman What can you do?
Sweeper Harriet, this is my world, and I want you out of it.
Harriet You were such a destructive boy yourself—broken windows and catapulted birds. Do you blame these for scratching where you're itching . . .? Mark time, dears, while we negotiate.

The groups mark time

Young Man Call yourself a policeman? Why don't you take her apart for causing a nuisance?
Sweeper I'm warning you . . .
Harriet What have I to do with the situation, dear boy? They're just waiting for the starting pistol. Hark.
A Guide Death or Glory.
A Broom King and Country.
A Guide Up the Revolution.
A Broom Down with Oppression.
A Guide Freedom and Democracy.
A Broom To the barricades.
A Guide Wipe out the enemy.
A Broom Give 'em cold steel.
A Guide Shoot 'em.
A Broom Bomb 'em.
A Guide Burn 'em.
A Broom Obliterate.
A Guide Destroy.
A Broom Destroy.
Guides and Brooms Destroy!
Sweeper (*shouting to make himself heard above the stamping feet*) That's enough!
Young Man They'll tear each other to bits.
Young Woman Peace. Remember?
Sweeper Fighting is forbidden. Understand? Fighting is out.
Harriet Don't be a spoil-sport. Let them have a jolly war if they want it.
Voices War, war, war. War, war, war.
Young Man We don't want a war.
Harriet Of course you do, dear boy. It's your chance to get away with murder.
Young Woman I'm a woman. It's no fun for me.
Harriet You haven't tried it, darling—kissing the boys good-bye before pushing them to the front.
Voices War, war, war. War, war, war.
Young Woman I don't want anybody to be hurt.
Harriet You need an interest in the casualty lists, darling. Else it's like watching a race without backing a horse. I've had lovers shot from under me in every major conflict.

Voices War, war, war. War, war, war.
Sweeper Cut it out.
Voices War, war, war.
Harriet Companeee—halt!
Voices One-two.

The groups stand to attention

Harriet Nothing like military training for obedience.
Young Woman Do you get the feeling that we're on the wrong side?
Young Man Should we swap?
Sweeper Don't you dare.
Young Woman If only you were better at your job.
Sweeper You watch. Right. Now you're all paraded, listen to me.
Young Woman Give it to 'em.
Sweeper Fighting is not only wrong—it's absurd. What do you get out of it but broken bones and broken lives? Of course every one of you thinks it always happens to the other chap. But it happens to somebody. Every orphan once had a father and mother. Every blinded man once had eyes. Every pile of rubble was once a building. And not theirs—yours. Now have you got all that into your silly noddles? War is bad for you. And what is more important—I don't like it. Now go home quietly, and lead contented lives. Thank you.

There is a polite patter of applause

Harriet My turn now. I am Aunt Harriet. *The* Aunt Harriet. I know I have the body of a woman, but I have the heart of a king, and a King of England, too. And gentlemen in England now abed shall think themselves accursed they were not here. With our backs to the wall we shall fight to the end. Give me liberty, or give me . . . Boots, to horse, saddle and away. Ours not to reason why. Shall we fight, or shall we fly? How can men die better than facing fearful odds? Are we downhearted? No. Let 'em all come. Cry "Havoc!" and let slip the dogs—would you live for ever? Up Guards and at 'em. Crying God for Harriet, England, and Saint George. (*She ends amid shouts and cheers*)

The Young Man and Young Woman shout, too, but the Sweeper soon stops them. He tries to make himself heard above the tumult, but fails. When there is a lull, the voice is Harriet's

Fall in!

The opposing groups sort themselves out into formation, facing each other

Young Woman Amazing.
Harriet Nothing to it, dear child. Action without responsibility. They're enjoying themselves. Heralds, banners, bugles, drums.

The music of a military tattoo begins. Heralds in brightly coloured surcoats appear, carrying banners. The groups march and counter-march. The Young Man tags on behind one column. The Young Woman tags on behind the other. The Sweeper pulls them out of the parade. He pushes them into a corner, then turns his attention to the marchers. He stands in front of a column, his hand raised like a policeman. The column knocks him down, and marches over him. When it has passed he staggers to his feet. The Young Man and Young Woman brush him down. He dashes back. This time he is bounced from one column to the next, and spun round and round. He totters away, giddy. The Young Man and Young Woman shake their heads, and cross to Harriet, who puts her arms around their shoulders. The Sweeper gestures wildly, indicating that the parade must stop. Nothing happens. Harriet blows a whistle. Immediate silence and stillness

> Battle stations.

Sweeper You two. Come back here.

Young Man Sorry.

Sweeper Respect, you promised. Co-operation, you promised.

Young Woman Peace, you promised.

Harriet Sensible darlings. If you can't avoid the battle, at least be on the winning side. Lined up to charge?

Sweeper I make the rules here. Either you stick to them, or you're done.

Harriet Darlings, you've been put-upon all your lives. Here's the chance to take it out on somebody else. Remember the whisperers, the sniggerers, the queue-jumpers, the form-pushers, the snobs, the louts. Bash, bash, bash. You'll feel so much better for it afterwards.

Sweeper You all want peace.

Harriet What's more, we'll fight for it. Last over the top's a cissy. On your marks . . .

Sweeper Oh, drop dead.

Harriet stands stock still for a second, then crumples. There is a momentary pause of incomprehension. Even the Sweeper is taken aback. The Young Man and Young Woman kneel by Harriet

Young Woman She is.

Young Man Did you . . .?

Sweeper I said . . .

An Indignant Person steps from the group

Indignant Person I say! You can't . . .

Sweeper (*without looking*) Drop dead.

The Indignant Person spins and drops. The groups draw together in a frightened bunch

> Just like that. A snap of the fingers, and . . . Just "Drop dead". Any questions? Any complaints? Any more for the Skylark? Remove these baubles.

The groups carry out the bodies

Young Woman You killed them.

Sweeper They made me angry,

Young Woman When you're angry you kill people?
Young Man You weren't angry with that other one. You didn't even look.
Sweeper So I don't even have to be angry. I just give the word. That's enough.
Young Man You're a killer.
Sweeper A creator. I run this show. Life and death: that's what it means. If I say "Go to the top of the class", you go to the top of the class. If I say "Bang"—you're dead.

The groups file back, heads bowed

Young Man And we trusted you.
Young Woman You're dangerous.
Sweeper You're never satisfied.

An Emissary from the group steps smartly forward, stands to attention, and salutes

Emissary Sir, permission to speak, sir.
Young Woman We know what we want.
Sweeper What anyone does for you, it's never enough.
Emissary Sir, permission to speak.
Young Man You don't even realize what you've done.
Young Woman You killed them.
Young Man Now you're hanging over us all like the bloody Bomb.
Emissary Sir, permission.
Sweeper You wanted peace, didn't you?
Young Man They're dead.
Sweeper Examples.
Young Woman You're supposed to set the example.
Emissary Sir.
Young Woman Ugh!
Young Man Get away.
Sweeper This is thanks.
Emissary Psst!
Sweeper You!

The Emissary shrieks and runs away

You're the nastiest, most ungrateful set of bipeds anybody had the misfortune to dream up.
Young Woman Oh, go and collect your thunderbolts.
Sweeper I might. I might do just that.
Young Woman You're a failure.
Sweeper All right. I'm a failure. Do you know what makes me a failure? You. You callous, treacherous, self-centred, cold-blooded, greedy, opinionated, lot. If I had a grain of sense, I'd wipe you out this minute. Where is that thunderbolt?

There is a lightning and thunder effect. The group fall to their knees

That's more like it. Let's have another.

Lightning and thunder effect. The group bow down with covered heads

Young Woman I hate thunder.
Sweeper Good.

Thunder. The group moans

Young Man I'll look after you. (*He puts his arm around the Young Woman*)
Sweeper More. Bigger. Better.

Lightning and thunder. The Young Woman falls to her knees

Young Man Don't worry. It never strikes in the same place twice.
Sweeper It strikes where I make it strike.

Lightning and thunder. The Young Man crouches by the Young Woman, covering her protectively. The group wails

Young Man Stop it, will you?
Sweeper Who's a failure?

Thunder

Young Woman We're sorry.
Young Man Are we?
Young Woman Right now we are.
Sweeper Once more for luck.

Thunder. The group's wails have now become a ritual. They lift up their arms, wail, and flop down

Group Lord, Lord. Spare us, Lord.
Sweeper Well, mind you behave yourselves.
Group Lord, Lord. We have sinned.
Sweeper All right. It's all over.
Group Lord, Lord. Forgive us, Lord.
Sweeper You can get up now.
Group Lord, Lord. We are dust.
Sweeper Yes, you're a miserable shower, but don't go on about it.
Group Lord, Lord, thy servants, Lord.
Sweeper This is going too far. It's embarrassing.
Group Lord, Lord. We bow down, Lord.
Sweeper I see you do. But I'm a modest person, with modest ambitions.
Group Lord, Lord. We praise thee, Lord.
Sweeper Just a little recognition. That's all I want.
Group Lord, Lord. We worship thee, Lord.
Sweeper A friendly smile, a raised hat, a wink, a nod, or a handshake.
Group Lord, Lord. We hearken to thee, Lord.

The group sits around the Sweeper, listening

Sweeper Not that I object to a little worship from time to time. I'm not
likely to give anybody seven days without the option on account of a

little worship. In fact, if a little worship makes you feel better, go ahead, and don't mind me. And if you feel like following it up with something a little more tangible, that's all right with me. The occasional devotional bowl of fruit, for instance, wouldn't come amiss; a sucking pig now and then, or a bottle of the local brew.

One of the group gets up and goes out. From time to time during the speech, others get up and go out

Mind you, I'm demanding nothing. There's no frustrated Chancellor of the Exchequer about me. But if you get a cosy glow from that odd personal sacrifice, then I won't refuse. In fact it would be appreciated. Mind you, I'm asking for nothing extortionate. I don't want to see anybody ruining themselves on my account. A tithe, say, would be quite sufficient. Of course, this ought to be properly organized. No point in having half a dozen fatted calves one week, and a dried prune the next. So some of you volunteer for the collecting. You can sort out the non-contributors at the same time. And don't let me catch anyone nicking anything on the side, or there'll be trouble. My word, yes. I'm not having anyone getting fat on my offerings. A tenth. That's right. One smart movement of the decimal point. And none of your second-rate produce, either—none of your old boiling fowls, your bruised fallings, your week-old fish, your sour wine. If the best is good enough for you, it's good enough for me. A little sacrifice is good for your moral fibre. It reminds you that there are higher things in life. Such as me. No, I'm not asking for much. Just a little regular worship. Once a week. It's a poor tale if you can't give up one day of the week to me. What's more I expect you to be properly dressed for parade— best blacks, shining faces, teeth brushed. And your mind on what you're doing. No cogitating on football pools during the service, working out how to stretch today's joint into tomorrow's casserole, or playing footsie with the young person adjacent. Such a lack of concentration is a mark of disrespect. And you'll do it willingly. If worship is not performed willingly, it is best not performed at all. I want to hear those voices raised. Because your half-hearted worshipper becomes your fully fledged backslider, and backsliding is something I do not care for. I want only true worshippers around me. So you can get rid of your backsliders and unbelievers as soon as you like. I don't care how. You don't expect me to waste good thunderbolts on them, do you? Hang them, shoot them, burn them, drown them. Publicly if necessary. As an example. I want my worship to be pure and unadulterated.

The last of the group gets up and goes out

The Sweeper looks around. Only the Young Man and Young Woman are left

Hey—where have they gone?

Young Man To find something else to worship.

Sweeper They can't.

Young Man Oh, it's quite easy. I'm always finding something new. When I was young I worshipped ice-cream: until I made myself sick—then I went on to the Beatles.

Sweeper I'm the one with the power of life and death in these parts.

Young Woman What has that to do with worship?

Young Man Any chap with a gun could claim as much, but nobody worships him. Let's face it—you're out of your depth in the god business.

Young Woman In fact you're not much good at anything, are you?

Sweeper I'm a jolly good sweeper.

Young Woman Everybody ought to be good at something.

Sweeper I've half a mind to go back to sweeping now.

Young Man I should if I were you.

Young Woman If you were good at it.

Young Man You stick to what you can do.

Young Woman I'd never have recommended being a god.

Young Man Not with your qualifications.

Young Woman I mean—sweeping up's one thing: organizing a complicated religion is quite a different pot of old incense.

Sweeper And what about the old thunder and lightning? (*He waves his hand*)

Thunder and lightning. The couple are quite unmoved

Young Woman You've seen one thunderstorm, you've seen them all.

Young Man That was your trouble.

Young Woman No variety.

Young Man No consumer research.

Young Woman No market surveys.

Young Man No wonder you didn't last.

Young Woman You didn't provide an up-to-date service.

Young Man Now they've taken their custom elsewhere.

Young Woman They're negotiating for another god.

Young Man Something more colourful.

Young Woman Flamboyant.

Young Man Inspiring.

Young Woman Personal.

Young Man Accommodating.

Young Woman Oracular.

Young Man Erotic.

Young Woman Get you. Consistent.

Young Man Spectacular.

Sweeper I said they can't, and I mean it. If they bring any of their false gods near me, I'll blast it and them to Kingdom Come.

Young Woman Where is Kingdom Come?

Sweeper Where they'll get blasted to, blast 'em. But they won't come back. They daren't.

Young Man Huh?

A noisy crowd is heard approaching, laughing, clapping, playing on pipes, tambourines, etc.

Sweeper Then just wait for fireworks.

The crowd enters. A procession of be-ribboned singers and dancers escorts a litter on which sits a great golden figure. It wears a stiff, intricate, vaguely Eastern costume and many jewels, particularly on its golden fingers. Its face is hidden by a heavy golden veil, almost like a curtain, attached to its pagoda-shaped headgear

Come on, then. Come here. Put it down. Let me have a good look.

The litter is set down

That? I wouldn't give it a penny for the guy. What is it supposed to do for you?

Voices Bring rain to our corn-fields.
Sun to our hay-fields.
Put the wind behind our team.
Turn it around at half-time.
Two cars to every garage.
And no traffic jams.
Wages up.
Prices down.
Pensions up.
Taxes down.
Bring babies.
Stop babies.
The god promises.

Sweeper No wonder you keep it veiled. Even if it's made of stone, it must be blushing. Well, before I smite it, let me see its face.

The God puts up a hand and tears away the veil

God Certainly, dear boy.
Sweeper Harriet!
Harriet *The* Harriet. Impressive, isn't it? I have all my window-dressing done by Harrods.
Sweeper That I can't forgive. You asked for trouble, and you'll get it. I'm going to wipe you out. Every one. We're going back to a nice, clean, bare stage—just as it was before I thought of any of you. Right. Now. (*He puts his hand over his eyes, and waves the other arm. He looks around. Everyone is still there, unmoving, silent, expectant*) Just one last piece of consideration, though you don't deserve it. I'll avoid humiliating you. I'll let you go theatrically.
A clap of thunder. Black-out. Gone. Right? Go!

Black-out and a clap of thunder

Lights.

Light returns. Everyone is still there

Obstinacy will get you nowhere. All right. If you want it the hard way, we'll see what an earthquake can do.

Lights flash on and off. There is a terrific rumble. But no-one moves

Landslide. Tidal wave. Hurricane. Water-spout.

The noise builds up and dies away. No-one moves

Harriet I'm sure you're building up to a terrific climax, dear boy. Do let us know when it's time to applaud.
Sweeper (*stunned*) You're still here.
Harriet There's only one thing that could move me—a really good cup of coffee. Or, after those atmospherics, even a bad cup of coffee. (*She claps her hands*) Acolytes—to the coffee-bar.

Her litter is lifted and she is borne to the exit. She tosses her veil to the crowd

Carry this, darlings. I can't bear living in a tent. (*She claps her hands*)

The litter bearers pause. Harriet turns to the Sweeper

Do join us, dear boy. I'm dying to have a chat. To tell the truth, I'm rather new to divinity. I'm sure you must have lots of wheezes. Can you find your own way up?

The litter is carried out, the crowd accompanying it

The Sweeper looks after it, dumbstruck

Young Man You *were* warned.
Sweeper You're only in my mind.
Young Woman Quite so. But as long as you've got a mind . . .
Sweeper You'll be here?
Young Woman Cheer up. We're not so bad really. She was right about the coffee. I need one, too. Coming, love?

Hand in hand, the couple walk out

Sweeper I do need a drink. If I were you, I'd get one, too. While there's a chance.

The Sweeper walks slowly out

The working Light comes on. The stage Lights fade. The house Lights come on

END OF ACT I

ACT II

The Sweeper returns with a cup of coffee and a sandwich. He sits eating and drinking

Sweeper Does this interest you? Watching a fellow human being masticate. Because if this fascinates you, spend a couple of hours in a Wimpy Bar. You'll have a ball. (*He finishes his drink and puts the cup down at the side of the stage*) I've got to stay to clear up, but you could have gone home. Some of you did. I daren't leave while that lot are on the loose. If I don't do something about them I'll be in dead trouble with The Manager. I'm only thankful he hasn't seen 'em. (*He looks up*) Have you noticed the lights? They went back to normal as soon as I left. There's a clue up there if only I had the brain to follow it. Perhaps...

The Lights change. The stage Lights come up, the auditorium Lights go down. The working Light goes off

Too late. I feel I've missed a chance.

The Young Man and Young Woman look in, see the Sweeper sitting all alone, and join him. Conversation starts in a desultory way

Young Woman Hi.
Sweeper You're not in the coffee bar, then.
Young Woman No.
Young Man We're here.
Sweeper I thought you'd be with them.
Young Man Them!
Young Woman We're not like them.
Young Man They're not like us.
Young Woman We're different.
Sweeper How?
Young Man Well...
Young Woman We're not in the coffee-bar.
Young Man They're in the coffee-bar.
Young Woman Having an orgy.
Sweeper In the coffee-bar? An orgy?
Young Woman She encourages orgies.
Sweeper Not in the coffee-bar!
Young Man Anywhere.
Young Woman That's the attraction of her religion. It's positive. There are no shalt-nots.
Sweeper I don't understand her.

Young Woman I find it reasonable. It's what I'd do if I were developing a religion. You can't think in the middle of an orgy. You can't brood over questions like "What am I doing here?" Once you do, the orgy's over. So you stay sky-high in wonderland—feeling like mad, but not thinking. She's a clever one, Harriet.

Sweeper But in the coffee-bar! I have to clean up there. It's bad enough after a matinée—but after an orgy! Bottle tops and toffee wrappers ... Why aren't you up there? Don't you enjoy orgies?

Young Woman We like to think for ourselves.

Sweeper That's what started this mess—you and your free will.

Young Man You started it. You made us.

Sweeper (*pointing at the Audience*) They started it. Out there. They tempted me. I fell.

*   *   *

The Young Man and Young Woman exchange shocked glances. They are suddenly very concerned

Young Woman Oh.

Young Man You're not good with temptations, then.

Sweeper Who is?

Young Man Oh.

Young Woman Then she'll hit what she's aiming for. Bull's-eye! Can I have the cuddly bear?

Young Man She might.

Young Woman She will.

Sweeper She?

Young Woman If you're not good with temptations.

Young Man She's a clever operator. Even if she were on the level, she'd be a menace. But she can tempt round corners.

Sweeper What's the big operation?

Young Man She wants you on her side.

Sweeper That's not even a joke.

Young Man You have the power, she has the glory. Together that's an unbeatable team.

Sweeper That's an outrage. An obscenity.

Young Woman She's revived the Seven Deadly Sins.

Sweeper That bunch of scarecrows?

Young Woman They're so attractive now. Oh, why do we keep backing you to win?

Young Man Your past performance does nothing to inspire confidence.

Sweeper You watch me. Let her come. (*Calling*) Harriet!

Young Woman Surely you don't want to see her this minute?

Sweeper Anything to get them out of that coffee-bar.

Young Man But you're not prepared for a fight.

Sweeper I'm not hanging about. It's not the drop that hurts, so much as the long, long walk to the scaffold.

Young Woman He's a barbarian at heart.

Sweeper (*shouting*) Harriet, you hag, let's be seeing you!

Harriet enters, riding on a decorated vehicle. She is dressed regally with crown, orb, sceptre, etc., and she sits on a throne. There is a vacant throne beside her. She is escorted by the Deadly Sins. Lust is a demure girl, prettily blushing. Gluttony is slender and elegant. Envy is a glowing pop star. Avarice is a smoothly successful businessman. Anger is a cheerful student demonstrator with a placard inscribed "Love, Honour, Obey". Sloth is in smart military uniform. No Pride

Harriet I've been waiting, dear boy. Don't loiter. Here's your throne.

Sweeper I'm not sticking my neck into anything.

Harriet You so persistently misunderstand. I'm the most well-meaning aunt in the world. I want everybody to be happy. I know what you want —deep, deep down.

Sweeper I've got everything I want.

Harriet That, dear boy, is an outright fib. I overheard what you whispered to Santa Claus. I do wish you'd let us help you.

Sweeper Us?

Harriet My activities are so far-flung I need assistants. These are my vice-chairmen and very dear friends. Your friends, too, darling. They're pining to meet you.

Sweeper As the shark said to the sardine.

Harriet (*with a wave to Lust*) Sweetheart, do try to convince the beast of our good intentions.

Lust shyly ventures towards the Sweeper

Lust I've waited so long for this moment.

Sweeper That's a conventional opening.

Lust I don't expect you to believe me, but I keep your photograph by my bedside—between my prayer-book and *A Hundred Things a Girl Should Know.*

Sweeper You're right. I don't believe you. Why should you keep my photograph?

Lust I have another. In a locket. It lies against my bosom. Oh, I shouldn't have said "bosom", should I? But here it is—look. (*She pulls out her locket, opens it, and shows him the picture*) It's warm. (*Replacing the locket*) Now you'll tell me I'm a little goose.

Sweeper I think you're a duck. I mean a chick. I mean . . .

Lust You're so much more attractive than your picture. It must be every girl's private dream to meet you. In the flesh. A girl needs an older man, doesn't she? Would you think me awfully pushing if I held your hand? (*She takes his hand*) You're so strong. (*She takes both his hands, looks into his eyes, and sighs*) I know a wood where bluebells grow.

Young Woman There he goes. Down at the first fence.

Sweeper What's your name, my dear?

Young Man Lust.

Sweeper Her—Lust? But she's so virginal.

Young Man There's many a good tune played on an old virginal.

Harriet My own invention, dear boy. Renewable virginity. Superfluous in my case, but a boon to millions. Selfless old Auntie.

Lust You do like me a little, don't you?

Young Woman Quick. Show Old Red-eyes a mirror.

Sweeper Me?

Young Man If only you could see yourself.

Harriet Take advantage of her if you feel inclined. She'll be just as dewy-fresh tomorrow.

Sweeper (*reluctantly*) I'll wait until tomorrow.

Lust Tomorrow, then. (*She blows a kiss, and runs into the arms of Envy*)

Young Woman Count to ten, and take a drink of cold water.

Young Man I still don't like the look in his eye.

Young Woman It's Envy.

Envy looks up

Envy Somebody call?

Harriet Superbly cued, my pet.

Sweeper You—Envy?

Envy No, man—you envy. (*Clicking his fingers at the Young Woman*) You, chick—available?

Hypnotized, the Young Woman goes to Envy and puts her arms around him

Pure formality. They're all available.

Young Man Hey!

He runs at Envy. Envy holds out his fist. The Young Man runs on to it, and collapses. Envy smiles at the Young Woman, and disengages himself

Envy Just for reassurance, baby. Testing the potential. (*Pushing a handful of notes at her*) For compensation. Buy yourself a Cadillac. (*Sprinkling notes over the Young Man*) Get another for supermate.

Sweeper You're—Envy?

Envy Whatever you want—I've got.

Harriet Pop star—millionaire—Universal Idol. He's collected so many golden discs he uses them for table-mats. And I'm his manager. Like to join us?

The Young Man groans. The Sweeper helps him to his feet

Young Man What hit me?

Sweeper Envy.

Young Man Let that be a lesson to you. (*Noticing the money*) What's this?

Sweeper Dandruff.

Harriet We're losing his attention. Avarice—action!

Avarice picks up the fallen notes

Avarice Excuse me, sir. Your property. Never leave money lying about.

Sweeper It's a temptation.

Avarice Oh, no. It can take root. There's nothing more inconvenient than money growing where you hadn't intended—like nasturtiums in the asparagus bed.

Sweeper Are you a gardener?

Avarice I have green fingers. Let me introduce myself. (*He holds out his hand*)

The Sweeper takes Avarice's hand

Avarice, sir. This year. Sir Avarice next: and I look forward to Lord Avarice. Not that titles really matter. They merely reflect the appreciation of my horticultural powers. The man who can make two dollars grow where only one grew before does more service to his country than the whole race of politicians. (*He realizes that he is holding the Sweeper's hand and breaks away*)

The Sweeper discovers a note sticking to his palm. Avarice takes it

A seed pound! Yes, indeed, a seed pound. In a year this will become a hundred: in a decade, a million.

Young Man How—how do . . .

Avarice You mean—do I take apprentices? I'm offering your friend a partnership. He can choose his own staff. Persuade him.

Young Woman Hey, you're on our side—remember?

Young Man But that money. All that money. We could buy the world.

Avarice (*horrified*) Buy? You said "Buy!"

Young Man That's what money's for—to spend.

Avarice Sacrilege! Do you grow roses to tear the flowers and scatter the petals? Money is meant to bloom, to be admired, caressed. Money should be loved for its own sake.

Young Man You have to live—to eat and sleep. How can you manage if you don't spend?

Avarice Credit, you philistine! You don't deserve to handle money. (*Snatching the notes from the Young Man and Young Woman*) Goths! Visigoths! Vandals!

Harriet He's going too far again. Mass, dears. Mass.

Lust and Envy pull away Avarice, who is still muttering, occasionally shouting, and almost foaming at the mouth. Gluttony, Anger and Sloth take his place

Three new playmates. Gluttony.

Gluttony, with a svelte figure, undulates down to the Sweeper

Gluttony I'm Gluttony.

Young Woman With that figure? I eat one potato, and it sticks out in front.

Gluttony With my slimming system you can gorge from breakfast to bedtime, and not show an ounce for it. Thick rich sauces, crusty new bread, ice-cream, nuts and fudge. Mouth watering? Bring your friend along,

The Young Woman puts a hand on the Sweeper's arm. The Young Man pulls her away

Young Man Don't you dare.

Gluttony Chocolate?

The Young Woman puts her hands over her face. The Young Man pats her shoulder

Young Man Don't fret. I'll still love you when you're sixteen stone.

Harriet Anger.

The student demonstrator steps forward

Anger (*full of compassion*) You poor, poor people. You don't know how to live. Love everybody. Pat the police dogs. They are our friends at heart, and only doing their duty. Bow to Authority. Authority knows what is good for you, and the Establishment acts for the best. Embrace everyone of all parties and creeds. The Kremlin is right, the Pentagon is right, the Pope is right, and all the thoughts of Chairman Mao. Welcome the tear gas and the baton charges. If a uniformed sadist hits you on the head, offer him your bottom. Inform on your neighbour that he, too, may be beaten and imprisoned, and so come to feel . . .

Sloth knocks him down

Kick me. Crush me. Revile me. I love your boots.

Harriet Sloth!

Sloth Ma'am.

Harriet Don't jump on him. We need him. He stirs up more trouble than the rest of you put together.

Sweeper Sloth?

Sloth (*jumping to attention*) Sir. Accidie, really. Spiritual sloth. It's a great life once you weaken. Nothin' to do but obey orders. And there's always somebody up there to give orders. You trade in your conscience when you draw the uniform. Nothin' like it for sweet, sound sleep.

Young Man It's a temptation.

Sweeper It's resistible. I'm not joining.

Harriet I'm not asking you to, dear boy. Come and take charge of them. All these beautiul people are so anxious to serve you.

Young Woman Here's the crunch.

Harriet Lust, Envy, Avarice, Gluttony, Anger, Sloth.

Sweeper There's one missing. Pride.

Harriet This throne was made to measure. It's waiting for you.

Sweeper Me?

Harriet Crown, orb, and sceptre, dear boy. I'm offering you control. Absolute control. That's what you want, isn't it? The command you lost. Here it is again. When you say "come", they'll come. When you say "go", they'll go. I trained them myself. Only a few steps to your throne.

Sweeper I could stop those orgies.

Young Man You only have to admit she's boss.

Young Woman It's a very small payment.

Sweeper Who's—what?

Harriet A mere title, dear man. What does the figure-head matter as long as the ship sails where you want?

Sweeper Nobody stands over me. Well—perhaps The Manager. But nobody here. None of you.

Harriet I hope you're not refusing.

Young Man He might. He might yet.

Harriet Are you leaving me with absolute control?

Sweeper No. You don't control me. You don't even control this pair. You only control suckers who fall for your soft sell.

Harriet I warn you . . .

Sweeper I've told you to drop dead before.

Harriet I'm a divinity now. Divinities don't drop dead.

Sweeper They only fade away. Well, fade, and take your bonus offers with you.

Harriet You can't order me. Or them.

Sweeper Think not? Here is a news flash. The Minister of Post and Telecommunications has just announced the formation of a National Commercial Radio Station. Ample opportunities for Avarice, Lust, Envy, Gluttony, Anger, and even Sloth. Jobs for everyone. Who will be the first to apply?

Sins Me. Me. Me. Me. Me. Me.

Jostling one another, the Deadly Sins rush off

Harriet I shan't forget this outrage. Afraid of trouble with The Manager, are we? There'll be orgies in the dressing-rooms, orgies in the wardrobe, orgies under the stage, orgies . . .

Sweeper I can feel a thunderstorm coming on. I'm still good with thunderstorms.

Harriet You can't scare me with thunderbolts.

Sweeper Have you ever seen velvet after a soaking? Was that a drop?

Young Woman I felt one.

Young Man There's another.

Sweeper And another.

Young Woman Faster.

Young Man Faster.

Sweeper Woosh!

Harriet dashes about trying to avoid the spots

Harriet An umbrella. Is there an umbrella in the house? My kingdom for an umbrella!

Harriet dashes off with her mantle over her head

Young Man Squark. Squark. Squark.

Young Woman Like a demented peacock jumping over puddles.

Young Man Pea-hen.

Young Woman Pea-hens don't have bright plumage.

Young Man I knew there was something odd about Harriet's sex.

Young Woman She's in full flight now.

Sweeper I beat her.

Young Woman Did you?

Sweeper Look—bright sun and a clear horizon.

Young Woman Wherever she is—preening her feathers and pretending it was all part of the act—there's a crowd gathering, too. Her following. Heil Harriet!

Sweeper It won't last for ever.

Young Man Optimist.

Sweeper Nothing lasts for ever.

Young Woman Pessimist.

Sweeper You dropped out.

Young Woman Ah. We're different.

Young Man We've got minds of our own.

*   *   *

Young Woman We had to drop out. We couldn't fight against the crowd, and we wouldn't run with it.

Sweeper So you came back to me.

Young Man Where else was there to go?

Young Woman A crowd's terrifying. You feel the pressure building up. You know that at any minute it's going to rush, to crush . . .

Sweeper And Harriet's in charge.

Young Woman Nobody's in charge. The mob's a great, blind monster. That's what really frightens me. Harriet isn't leading. She's just very good at working out where the crowd is going next. She uses a computerized psephology department: nobody could guess right ten times out of ten—especially somebody out of your mixed-up subconscious. She ensures that, whichever way the mass points, she's out front.

Sweeper You have to take your hat off to that woman.

Young Man A real leader would knock spots off her.

Sweeper Think so?

Young Man That crowd is ripe for a leader. The right man at the head would make Genghis Khan look like a Brown Owl. He'd have the world in his hand.

Sweeper What job are you doing right now?

Young Man I'm associated with the Ministry of Social Security. I help to justify its existence.

Sweeper Ever thought about the King business?

Young Man Not seriously. I'm short of qualifications. My dad's blood wasn't blue. His language sometimes, but not his blood.

Sweeper I've got influence.

Young Man What's the proposition?

Sweeper Help me to keep them in order, and I'll push you to the top.

Young Woman Can you?

Sweeper Do as you're told, remember I'm boss, and the world is yours. Keep me established, and I'll keep you established.

Young Man Where do we start?

Sweeper All you have to do is stand up, and proclaim yourselves.

Young Woman Oh King, live for ever?

Young Man Hail King. Live for ever.

Sweeper Make it convincing.

Young Woman Shall we take the risk—your majesty?

Young Man What have we got to lose?

Young Woman Don't remind me. You know what happens to failed royalty. Thud!

Sweeper That's not an attitude of reverence.

Young Woman Sorry.

Young Man On the beat.

Young Woman One, two.

Young Man
Young Woman ⎫ You are the right, true and only. ⎬ (*Speaking together*)

Sweeper Sound as though you meant it.

They raise their arms and bow

Young Man
Young Woman ⎫ You are the right, true and only. ⎬ (*Speaking together*)

Sweeper You'll look better when you dress the part. There's a wardrobe behind the scenes. Help yourselves to a couple of costumes. Come back looking like Leaders.

The Young Man and Young Woman exit chanting "O King, Live for Ever"

[*If the "Deadly Sins" section has been cut, at this point the Sweeper sets up two thrones*]

Pretty shoddy material, but they're all I've got to work with. Anyway, with me to clear the way, they can't go far wrong. First the softening-up process. Harass Harriet with a few natural disasters. Nothing serious, mind you. The up-against-it attitude is a godsend to any government. What people can't stand is getting their feet wet. Let's start with a soaking summer—the final test washed out. Then a strike of television engineers—nothing to do in the evenings but look at each other. A mild epidemic of Oriental flu, and a plague or so of rodents. Can you hear a muttering? The muttering grows to a grumbling. The grumbling grows to a mighty rumbling, and . . .

Harriet appears, furious

Harriet Ah! You're doing it.

Sweeper You're a divinity. Can divinities be frightened by mice?

Harriet They can be irritated by incompetents. I'm a better divinity than you any day.

Sweeper You'll learn, Harriet. Even if it has to be the hard way. This is *my* world.

Harriet Sssh, dear one. Somebody might hear. Do you want them to laugh? Hark.

Harriet's followers enter, saluting and shouting

Crowd Heil, Harriet! Heil, Harriet! Heil, Harriet!

Harriet leaves the Sweeper and takes up a commanding position

Harriet My people!

Crowd Harriet!

Harriet Yes, my darlings. I know you suffer, but I am suffering with you. Your pleasures are my pleasures, and your tragedies my tragedies. Your Harriet loves you.

Crowd Harriet!

Sweeper Now where are my candidates?

Crowd Harriet for ever!

Sweeper They should be dressed by now.

Crowd We love Harriet!

Sweeper Where are they?

Crowd Harriet! Harriet! Harriet!

Sweeper Oh, come as you are.

A fanfare is heard above the noise. The crowd falls silent

About time, too.

In silence, the Young Man and Young Woman enter and mount to their thrones. They are dressed in barbaric splendour, but are nervous behind their imperial trappings

Harriet Who are you?

Young Man (*his voice uncertain under the strain*) My name is Adam, King of Kings.

Harriet Children, playing.

Young Man Bow before us.

Sweeper Good boy. But louder.

Young Man Pay homage.

Harriet Unconvincing.

Sweeper Louder.

Young Man Kneel.

Harriet Put your toys away.

Young Man Prostrate yourselves.

Sweeper I said louder.

Young Man (*in a drill sergeant's thunder*) Obey!

Sweeper Long live the King!

Crowd Long live the King!
Voice in Crowd Long live the King!

Over the heads of the Crowd the Young Man gestures to the Sweeper—
"What now?" The Sweeper gestures for silence. The Young Man repeats
his gesture. The Crowd falls silent

Young Man I am your King.
Crowd Long live the King!
Young Man Show me.

The Crowd kneels

Harriet Fools!

The Crowd turns to Harriet. The Young Man looks at the Sweeper, who can-
not think of the next move

You took long enough to find your freedom—to break away from yon
blunderer with his whims and tantrums, his musts and must-nots. I
led you from bondage. Are you lusting again for strait-jackets? No?
Then come to your Harriet.

The Crowd gets up and surges round Harriet

Crowd Harriet for ever! Harriet for ever!

Harriet points to the bewildered Young Man and Young Woman

Harriet Tear them down!

The Crowd attacks the Young Man and Young Woman

Young Woman Help!
Crowd Tear them down! Tear them up! Tear them to pieces!

The Young Man and Young Woman stand on their thrones, and keep the
attackers at bay by using their regalia as weapons. The Sweeper is out of his
depth again

Young Woman Don't just stand there.
Young Man Read the Riot Act.
Young Woman Fire over their heads.
Young Man You got us into this.
Young Woman You get us out.
Harriet Your serve.
Sweeper Midges. Gnats. Fleas. Ticks. Pin-prickers. Pimple-raisers.

The Crowd forgets its attack as it slaps and scratches

Wasps. Hornets. Buzzers. Stingers.
Harriet You shall smart for this.
Sweeper You're the smart one, Harriet. Tell them, sonny-boy.
Young Man We are your King. We are . . . We . . .
Young Woman (*shouting*) They can't hear for these damned flies!
Sweeper Insects out!

The Crowd realizes that the plague has stopped. As relief spreads they notice the Young Man standing with his arms raised. Silence

Young Man You have raised your hands against us. Rebelled against us. Against your King.

The Crowd groans

Young Woman Your King.
Crowd Our King. Our King.
Harriet Any fool can claim a crown: it takes a king to wear one. Where are their credentials?
Young Man We were appointed.
Young Woman Anointed.
Young Man By the right, true, and only.
Harriet What have they ever done for you?
Young Woman We slew the pests.
Harriet A public health officer could have done as much.
Young Woman You didn't.
Harriet I am a divinity—not a disinfectant. I am Harriet. The genuine and unrepeatable Harriet.
Crowd Harriet! Harriet!

Crowd surges round Harriet

Young Woman They're so fickle.
Young Man Let's drop this king lark.
Sweeper There's only one way out for you. (*He brings his hand down like an axe*) Thud!
Young Man Ouch!
Young Woman Me, too.
Sweeper Give them an enemy. There's nothing like a war to rally support. Smite the Philistines!
Young Woman I thought you were against wars.
Sweeper A war on my side is a just war.
Young Man My people!
Harriet *His* people!
Young Man I turn to you in this dark hour of trial.
Harriet Dark? Trial? Is this your economic miracle?
Young Man Ever the envy of less-happy lands, this dear country to which we owe so much is in peril. Even now, the invader threatens. With heavy heart we proclaim that war is inevitable. Our heart is laden, but our head is unbowed. We put our trust in you—loyal subjects, countrymen, friends. We know you stand unflinchingly behind your sovereign.
Crowd Our King. Long live the King!
Harriet Turn back to Harriet before you're skinned alive!
A Lone Voice Harriet!
Young Man Who shouts for Harriet?
Crowd He did.
A Lone Voice No, I didn't.

Young Man There may be some with objections to this holy war.

Young Woman We are dedicated to upholding liberty of conscience.

Young Man There may be some who would like to shake hands with the enemy.

Young Woman You have freedom to think what you will.

Young Man There may be some who would stand by while our homes are burned, our treasures looted, our women raped.

Young Woman Oh!

Young Man There may even be some who gamble on rewards from a triumphant aggressor. Are any such here—of these grubs, these caterpillars, destroying what they fatten on? If there are any such—speak. Shout Harriet!

Harriet Harriet!

Young Man Traitor!

Harriet I'm a law unto myself, dear boy. You can't touch me.

Young Woman Can't we?

Sweeper You *can* turn her out.

Young Man We banish Harriet. Let no-one consort with her, give aid or comfort, or succour her. From this time forth let Harriet be neither seen nor spoken of in this realm. Begone, Harriet!

Harriet smiles and folds her arms

Harriet Now show who's boss.

The Young Man is nonplussed again

Sweeper You're in charge, and I'm behind you.

Young Man I speak in the name of the right, true, and only. There is the Enemy. Drive her out!

Crowd Out! The Enemy! Out with her!

The Crowd surges towards Harriet. She halts them with a raised hand, and turns to the Sweeper

Harriet You never did learn to look ahead, dear boy. You invented the Enemy, did you? Well, now you have one.

Harriet sweeps out. Shouting and jeering, the Crowd rushes off after her

TThe Young Man and Young Woman come down from their thrones and join the Sweeper

Young Man Whew!

Young Woman That was close. If people were meant to be torn apart, they'd come with perforations.

Young Man How long can we keep it up?

Sweeper Toe the line, and you could rule as long as the Pharaohs. Incidentally, you'd better *start* a line. A Royal Family needs a family. Do you want me to write it in for you?

Young Woman No, thanks. We can do some things for ourselves.

Sweeper Oh, I wouldn't deprive you of your ante-natal joys—just fix the results. True Family Planning. A boy for the heir-apparent. A girl for the Royal Wedding—pageantry without politics. And another boy in case of accidents. That suit you?

Young Man Sounds feasible.

Sweeper Good. . . One year later.

A baby cries, off

Two years.

A baby cries, off

Three years later.

A baby cries, off

You're established.

Young Woman I'm exhausted.

Sweeper Now—if you don't mind my mentioning it—the other half of the bargain.

Young Man (*off-handedly*) Oh, that. You are the right, true, and only.

Sweeper As long as you don't forget it. I'm not throwing my weight about —that's your job. I don't care how you manage the business, but make it run smoothly—without orgies, riots, or demonstrations. Draw up a set of regulations—no smoking on stage, no chips in the dressing-rooms, and last man out switch the lights off. That sort of regulation. Tell 'em I okayed the orders, and if anyone breaks 'em, there'll be trouble with the right, true, and only. If there's any real trouble, give me a call. Only don't call too often. I've got to work out a good story to tell The Manager when he turns up. (*He sits down at the side of the stage in an attitude resembling Rodin's "Thinker"*)

Young Woman Just a minute.

Sweeper Mmm?

Young Woman What happens to us if you're thinking about something else?

Sweeper Let's find out. You're in charge. You know the way I want things done. Just carry on as though I were with you and watching.

Young Woman Aye-aye, sir.

Sweeper But be quiet about it.

A Messenger runs on stage shouting, and falls on his knees in front of the Young Man

Messenger Sire! Sire! The Enemy!

Sweeper Quiet!

Young Woman Shush.

Messenger (*in a stage whisper*) The Enemy.

Young Man (*whispering*) The Enemy? Where?

The Messenger mimes someone rowing towards the shore

Young Woman (*whispering*) What enemy?

The Messenger mimes someone tall, busty, and wielding a weapon

Young Man Britannia?

The Messenger shakes his head

Young Woman Harriet!

The Messenger nods, and mimes rowing. The Young Man holds up one finger. The Messenger shakes his head, and goes on rowing. The Young Man holds up two fingers. The Messenger shakes his head, and indicates other boats behind. The Young Man holds up both his hands. The Messenger stops rowing and shows his fingers repeatedly. He does it so often it becomes a nervous tic. The Young Woman holds his hands to stop him. The Young Man makes for the Sweeper, but the Young Woman holds him back. She mimes shooting—first with pistols, then with a rifle, then with a machine-gun. She waves a hand at an imaginary cleared field. The Messenger nods enthusiastically, and is about to go, but the Young Man beckons him back. The Young Man points to the Sweeper, puts his fingers in his ears, and shakes his head. The Young Woman considers, then mimes shooting with a bow and arrow

The Messenger shakes his hands over his head, and runs out

The Young Man flexes his muscles, mimes drawing a sword, and slashes with it

The Messenger staggers back with an arrow sticking through him, and indicates hordes pursuing him. The Messenger staggers off again

The Young Man kisses the Young Woman, then brandishes his sword

Young Man In the name of the right, true, and only.

The Sweeper, without looking, waves a vague acknowledgement

The Young Man marches off to deal with the Enemy

The Young Woman watches him go, wipes away a tear, then turns to the Sweeper

Young Woman Did you see that?

But the Sweeper is now talking to the Audience

Sweeper Perhaps if I could get rid of you lot . . . I'm sure there's something good on television—a re-run of last week's match in slow motion, that film you've always meant to catch and always missed, another repeat of *The Forsyte Saga*.

Young Woman You . . .

Sweeper Just file in an orderly manner towards the exits. No? Oh.

The Messenger runs back with two arrows sticking in him. He indicates a battle raging off-stage, realizes that he is wounded, and staggers off again

Young Woman (*turning to the Sweeper*) All right. We'll have to learn to do without you. We'll stand on our own feet, or go under.

Sweeper Eh? Be careful with your blood-baths. The Manager's very particular about his paintwork.

Young Woman It's going to be a long war.

Sweeper He's sure to be back, soon. He practically lives in the theatre. Up there in his office. Balancing the books.

Young Woman What's more, the enemy is cruel and beastly, and stoops to practices no civilized being could imagine this side of madness.

Sweeper You've got to win. Why do you think I promoted you?

Young Woman Then we must become crueller, and beastlier, and stoop even lower. That's the trouble with war: it's so damned corrupting. This very minute, to get information, they're torturing our prisoners. But we can't hear the cries above the screams of their prisoners.

Sweeper Oh, no.

Young Woman Not cricket? My dear, sweet soul, there's no such thing as a clean war. Death is death—whether one death or millions. Death is death, whether cock-of-the-walk or frightened old woman. And the most corrupting thing about war is that, in the end, it ceases to be anything. We can talk about the cruelty and beastliness just as calmly as I am talking now.

Sweeper You're—changing.

Young Woman I doubt if the change is for the better.

The Messenger staggers in, bristling with arrows like a hedgehog. He is completely confused and makes vague gestures

Do you mean we lost?

The Messenger makes vague gestures and staggers off again

(*Turning to the Sweeper*) Trust you to muck everything up. Next time fight your own battles.

Sweeper But I'm on your side.

Young Woman Perhaps you'd have been more use to us on theirs. Look.

Two grim soldiers enter. They halt, come to attention, and order arms

Well, what is it to be? Hanging, beheading, shooting? Get on with it. I haven't time to waste.

The Young Man marches with authority between the soldiers, who present arms

The Young Woman looks at him for a second, then runs into his arms

We won! We won!

Sweeper What else did you expect?

Young Woman But he had his mind on something else all the time.

Young Man That helped. He has very old-fashioned ideas. Now we really start to rule.

He leads the Young Woman up to the throne

Wait for it.

A fanfare. The Crowd enters, respectfully

Victory!

The Crowd cheers

The Enemy has been defeated!

Sweeper Of course, with me behind you . . .

Young Man It was a hard and bitter fight .

Sweeper You could rely on me.

Young Man But the Enemy has not been destroyed. The Enemy is still watching, still waiting. We must always be on our guard.

Sweeper Now a few words of thanks to the right, true, and only.

Young Man Safety lies in obedience. In right thinking. In clean, sober, industrious living. In doing what is best for you without question.

Sweeper Quite so, but a few . . .

Young Man We want to keep you safe.

Sweeper I said a few words of thanks to the . . .

Young Man So we have appointed deputies to help you.

Sweeper A few thanks to . . .

Young Man There are deputies to tell you what to do, and deputies to tell you what to think.

Sweeper I say . . .

Young Man There are deputies to tell me what you are thinking.

Sweeper Hey!

Young Man Remember, it is for your own good.

Sweeper You—tell him.

A Voice in the Crowd I fought for freedom.

Young Man That is a dangerous thought.

The Voice Is freedom unlawful?

Young Man Dangerous thoughts lead to unlawful thoughts.

The Voice In the old days we did as we liked. Thinking was free.

Young Man Take care.

The Voice I want to go back to the free old days.

Young Man Go then. Take him back.

The two soldiers hustle out the heckler

That is a germ of doubt, a germ of rebellion. One germ can start an epidemic. Let us have no plagues.

Shots are heard, off

Sweeper You can't do that.
Young Woman Who says?
Sweeper Me. The right, true, and . . .
Young Man (*addressing the Crowd*) To celebrate our achievements there will be a mass execution at mid-day. Everyone assemble in the Municipal Square. And no absentees.
Sweeper Listen to me. All of you.

The Sweeper's voice is drowned by a fanfare

The Crowd hastily disperses

The Young Man and Young Woman come down to the Sweeper

Young Man Let's keep our squabbles to ourselves.
Sweeper Executions! I won't have it.
Young Man You haven't the choice, old man. We're in charge.
Sweeper I put you there.
Young Man Sure. We give you the credit.
Young Woman We always shout "In the name of the right, true, and only".
Young Man Before the axe falls.
Young Woman So you're in it with us..
Young Man The secret police.
Young Woman The midnight knock.
Young Man The interrogation room.
Young Woman "In the name of the right, true, and only!"
Young Man Thud!
Sweeper You little horrors . . .
Young Woman We don't see it quite that way.
Young Man We've taught the crowd to shout "O King, live for ever." I don't suppose we shall, but I've got our scientists working on the problem.
Young Woman You want them kept in order, don't you? For your sake we have to stay on top.
Sweeper This isn't my way. You'll open the prisons, disband the secret police, and burn the scaffolds. As of now, or I withdraw my support.
Young Man Why don't you go and look out for your Manager?
Sweeper Don't you come the old Harriet with me. You're not immortal. Kings have had accidents.
Young Woman Then our little boy will be King. Oh, you haven't met our family, have you? You'll love the children.
Young Man You should see them pulling the wings off flies.

A cheer is heard, off

Young Woman Are they starting the ceremony without us?
Young Man Heads will roll if they do.

They hurry to the exit

Young Woman Please don't worry about the executions.

Young Man They're really necessary.
Young Woman And they can be such fun.

The Young Man and Young Woman exit

Sweeper (*shouting after them*) Children. That's all you are. Children. Pulling the wings off flies.

A drumroll, off, suddenly cut off. A cheer. Miserably the Sweeper turns back

Was I just talking to myself? They're not real. They're only figments of my imagination. Something I invented. Imagination.

Off, a roll of drums and a cheer

I didn't hear that. I won't invent any more. It'll only go wrong anyway. I won't be drawn into any dream world. I won't.

Off, a scream, followed by a cheer

But how else can they be kept in order? Leave them to themselves, and they'll go from bad to worse. I need somebody to help me. Somebody temptation-proof. Somebody devoted to my interests. Somebody incorruptible.

The Girl enters, cool and stately in a white robe

Who are you? Yes, that's the way, whiter than white with the powerful new ingredient—sanctity. (*He laughs, but his laugh turns into a cough*) Hell, I can't make cracks. They dry in my throat, and turn into croaks. You're a disturbing influence, and too innocent to know what you're disturbing. I never realized my imagination could soar so high. Really a man ought not to feel this way about his own creation—it's almost incestuous . . . Go to them, Girl. They need you. Bring them back to my ways.

The Girl goes up to the throne

Wait, though.

The Girl turns

Be careful. You're only human. Bones can be broken; blood can be spilt. You can be hurt; you can die. Be careful. Roused man's a dangerous animal. (*He turns from her, and continues to address her, but with his back to her*) Humanity can't cope with purity at the best of times. Distilled water, pure oxygen, absolute alcohol—they're out for all normal purposes. The human carcass is germ-laden, and subject to adulteration. What the human soul is like doesn't bear investigation. Pure goodness hits that heap of corruption like a blast of radiation. So take care of yourself. I know what you do to me . . . But I don't have to tell you anything. You even know the crooked game I'm playing.

Yet you're above it all, like moonlight on the mountain-tops. (*He turns and hurries to her*) It is necessary, you know. If The Manager should . . . There's not much time left. (*Suddenly, he kneels and kisses the hem of her robe*)

The Girl smiles and strokes his head. He jumps up and strides away from her

Does a bomb know what its purpose is? Or what happens when it's detonated? Does it care?

The Girl stands between the two thrones, waiting

The Young Man and Young Woman enter with Court Officials and Guards

Young Woman (*angrily*) The worst execution I ever saw. Who was the director? No, don't tell me. Just gut him tomorrow.
Young Man And there were murmurs.
Young Woman Murmurs?
Young Man When we arrived, and when we left. Murmurs.
Court Official Oh, not murmurs, sire.
Young Man I heard murmurs. I'm sensitive to murmurs.
Court Official Low cheers, perhaps.
Young Man Murmurs.
Court Official Suppressed coughing, maybe.
Young Man Murmurs.
Court Official Of appreciation, sire.
Young Man (*shouting*) Bloody, disgruntled, let's-get-rid-of-'em-type murmurs. Deal with them.
Court Official To hear is to obey.
Young Woman It had better be.

The Young Man and Young Woman turn towards their thrones. They see the Girl and freeze. The Court Official hurries up to the Girl

Court Official What are you doing in the Holy of Holies? Where's your pass? Why aren't you in uniform? (*Uncertainly*) Consider yourself under arrest. Anyone who . . . (*His voice trembles and fails*) Who . . .?
Young Woman A clear breach of security.
Court Official O King, live for ever . . .
Young Man There has been an alien rear on our throne.

The Girl indicates the empty throne, walks down to the Young Man and Young Woman, and kneels

Young Woman Don't mention it.
Young Man Accept our Royal Thanks for allowing us to sit on our own flaming throne.

The Girl rises. The Young Man tries to cut her down to size with sarcasm, but under her cool gaze, fumbles and dries

Those seats are sacred—understand? Consecrated to these seats. Oh,
Hell!

Young Woman (*trying where he has failed*) That long, cool look is reserved
for . . . In underlings it is . . .

Court Official What is to be done with the Young Person, sire?

Young Man Done?

Young Woman Done! Guards!

First Guard Ma'am.

Young Woman Take her away.

First Guard What then, ma'am?

Young Man Do what you like with her.

The Guard grins

Young Woman And I hope she enjoys it.

With a lewd laugh the Guard approaches the Girl. His laugh dies

First Guard If you wouldn't mind coming this way, miss. . . .

Young Man What got into him? Corporal!

The Second Guard strides to the Girl, and gets the full blast of her personality

Second Guard We'll just make sure you're all right as far as the gate,
miss.

First Guard Some very rough characters in these parts.

The two Guards gently escort the Girl out

Young Man Since when have eunuchs been recruited into the Palace
Guards?

Young Woman Which Guards let her in?

Young Man Find out.

Young Woman Promptly.

Young Man Follow up with a Court Martial.

Young Woman Also promptly.

Young Man We want to hear the firing squad before sundown.

Court Official To hear is . . .

Young Man Move!

The Court Official runs out

Young Woman When she looks into you, she sees that insignificant beetle
—the real you.

Young Man I don't sleep well. She took advantage of my insomnia.

Young Woman How did she get in?

The Young Man points to the Sweeper

Young Man He's working again.

Young Woman That back number? We're independent now. Since U.D.I.
we have been the spiritual heads of the community.

Young Man We are the right, true, and only.

Young Woman So don't hang about. You're an anachronism.
Young Man You're not needed.
Sweeper I'm waiting.
Young Woman You planted that little upstart, didn't you? Just as you did us. But we know that trick. I'd take her away, if I were you.
Young Man Because we are absolute rulers, and we mean to stay that way. We can be very brutal.
Sweeper I think you're very frightened. I can afford to wait a little longer.
Young Man You won't like it. (*Shouting*) Summon our Adviser!

Diminishing shouts of "Adviser", off

Where is the Adviser?
Harriet (*off*) Coming, dear boy.

Harriet enters briskly. Her appearance now has something Satanic about it

Sweeper But she's the Enemy.
Young Man Set a thief, to coin a phrase.
Young Woman If you can't beat 'em, as the commercial goes.
Harriet Satan finds some mischief still, as the poet says. (*She takes up a position behind the Young Man and Young Woman*)
Young Woman I wish you'd stand where we can see you.
Harriet The power behind the throne, dear heart. Now, this crisis . . .
Young Man They're thinking. There are signs of it everywhere. We have imposed censorship, suppressed the living word, reduced television to pop, pap, and propaganda; but still they're thinking. And we don't know what.
Harriet You're not as experienced as you imagine, dear ones. Give the darlings something to occupy their minds, then you'll know what their minds are occupied with.
Young Woman Such as?
Harriet A persecution.
Young Man Public buildings are bristling with discarded heads.
Harriet That was your private persecution. Now you need a campaign that anyone can join in. Give them all a chance to dance in blood.
Sweeper If you listen to her, you'll be sorry.
Harriet (*ignoring him*) Just pick a section of the community you can do without, and let rip. What shall it be—red beards? Warts? Wigs?
Young Woman That's not logical.
Harriet There is nothing logical about persecution. Logic is a disadvantage. It could lead to flash-back.
Young Woman Flash-back?
Harriet Let's not worry about flash-back at this stage. Just give your hounds the scent and turn them loose.
Young Man Call the Chief of Police.
Harriet Police!
Young Woman There's no need to shout. His ear's at the keyhole.

The Chief of Police enters. He is wearing a white robe and peaked cap, and carries a flower in his hand

Chief of Police Sire! (*He salutes*)

Young Man What garb is that?

Chief of Police Oh, everyone's wearing them.

Young Man You were issued with buttons and badges. You will display brass buttons and badges. Dispose of that bath-robe.

Chief of Police Here, sire?

Young Man In private.

Chief of Police (*saluting*) Sire!

Young Man Bring us the file on social undesirables.

Chief of Police But, sire, there are no social undesirables.

Young Woman Have we wiped out the lot?

Chief of Police In the easiest way. Now we love them. We love everyone. So everyone is desirable.

Young Man Everyone?

Chief of Police Even you, sire.

Young Man Could we begin by persecuting the police?

Harriet Not a good idea. I prefer the police on my side.

Chief of Police It's the Girl, sire. To see me now, you wouldn't think I was once an uncouth, intemperate, irascible sort of fellow, would you? Oh, please say that you wouldn't. But I was. Then I saw the Girl. Or rather she saw me. She saw the splendid chap I was deep down inside. She didn't say a word, but I was filled with a warm glow as from a generous measure of confiscated over-proof spirit. Then I understood the others.

Young Woman The others?

Young Man That Girl! So she was the ace up your sleeve, you butter-mouthed rumble-gut.

The Sweeper shrugs innocently

Young Woman Never mind the Girl for now. The others!

Chief of Police She cut a swathe of brightness through our sordid metropolitan life. Wherever she walked radiance hung about. Thieves stopped thieving; hypocrites stopped canting; whores gave themselves for love; and wrath ran away down the gutters. Trust blossomed, prices tumbled, and production soared.

Young Man Stop! We'll have a revolution on our hands.

Chief of Police Not a revolution, sire. A revelation.

Young Woman That's worse. We are the right, true, and only. We. Us.

Young Man To fall under any other influence is treason.

Young Woman Arrest that bitch!

Chief of Police Sire, I'd sooner arrest myself.

Young Man Then arrest yourself.

Chief of Police As sire wishes. (*He salutes. He is about to withdraw when he realizes that he is still holding the flower. He presents it to the Young Man*) To sire, with love.

The Chief of Police salutes and marches out

The Young Man paces furiously

Young Man Hooks and pincers! He shall die by millimetres.

Young Woman So will you if you don't calm down. Your ulcers.

The Young Man tries to tear the flower to pieces, but it is too tough for him

Young Man It's defiance! It's bloody-minded, wanton, deliberate, indefensible defiance. (*He throws the flower to the ground and jumps on it*)

Harriet Temper, temper. Reserve the histrionics for your public appearances. (*She picks up the flower*) Pretty.

Young Man It was an insult. "Stick this in your buttonhole", he was saying. And I discovered him. He was just another knuckle-dusting, bicycle-chaining yob when I took him into the force. I promoted him over the heads of milder men. And now he dares to—to . . .

Sweeper That's the way it goes.

Young Man To glow at me. Offers flowers. If she could do that to him . . .

Harriet One should always say thank you for a gift.

Young Man I do not want flowers.

Harriet I mean the gift from that has-been in the corner. An ideal object for persecution. We can kill several birds with one stone.

Young Woman I'd rather kill one bird with several stones.

Harriet That can be managed, too.

Sweeper You wouldn't dare. That Girl is under my protection.

Young Woman We all know what that's worth. Her white robe is going to get very, very dirty.

Sweeper Let's try diplomacy. I don't want that Girl to be harmed. Name your price.

Young Woman How do we begin? A proclamation?

Harriet Nothing so crude. A whisper is enough. How obliging of the darlings to provide identification. We'll generate a splendid head of prejudice with white robes.

Sweeper You won't touch that Girl. You tried once, and failed.

Harriet A mob is different. A mob has neither humanity, mercy, nor pity. A mob has a hundred heads, one voice, and no heart.

Young Woman Let it loose!

Sweeper I've warned you. What happens hereafter you bring upon yourselves.

Harriet We'll discuss the cost after we've counted the bodies.

Harriet goes out

Sweeper Do you want a massacre of innocents?

Young Man You name the game.

Young Woman We'll play it.

The Young Man and Young Woman follow Harriet

Sweeper And down goes the bait. But this is the difficult part. I know what's happening off-stage, but I must stand here, and let it happen. The plan has to work by itself or it won't work at all. I have to trust her. I feel with her. I can hear the scurrying of feet down side-streets and alleys, with the occasional cry of an unfortunate caught up in the works. Then I see them—wave after wave of glassy eyes and slack mouths. I could run, but they're behind, too—a closing circle. Why should I run? I hurt nobody. And, for a while, innocence holds back the flood. The old spell works on a few. The wolves become human again. Their eyes are bewildered. What are they doing? For a while, silence. Nightmare silence, heavy with the stench of the monster's breath. At last the monster roars: the death scream of the mob. Then terror and pain as flesh yields and tears. Darkness, like the monster's mouth, gapes and swallows. (*He turns away and hides his face*)

A cheering, laughing, dancing, drunken crowd invades the stage. Harriet leads on the Young Man and Young Woman. They mount to their thrones and sit

Harriet takes up her position behind them. She now overshadows them, seeing the suffering Sweeper, and enjoying her moment of triumph. This is now all hers. She laughs

The Girl enters, covering her face with her hands. She goes to the Sweeper, who puts an arm round her paternally, and consoles her

A torn, bloodstained robe is brought on, and held up. Gradually the hysteria dies, and the crowd falls silent

Don't cry, my dear. You didn't fail me. Every part of the plan clicked into place. Look.

The robe is thrown to the ground. It lies in the centre of the stage. The Crowd draws back in horror

A Voice in the Crowd They did it!

The cry is picked up: "They did it! They did it!" Accusing fingers begin to point until the whole Crowd is pointing at the thrones crying: "They did it!" The Young Man and Young Woman shrink back in guilt and horror. Then they rise. The Crowd falls back as the Young Man and Young Woman stumble down from their thrones. The Young Man and Young Woman turn and point at Harriet

Young Man / Young Woman She did it! (*Speaking together*)
Crowd She did it!
Young Man / Young Woman Cast her out! *Speaking together*)
Sweeper For ever?
Crowd For ever. And ever.

Harriet is seized and whirled from one member of the Crowd to another until she is opposite the Sweeper

Harriet You win. You'll stretch out their guilt, and tie them into knots with it. They're all yours. You win.

Sweeper I was bound to, Harriet. I wrote the script.

Harriet But who is writing yours, dear boy?

Harriet sweeps out

The Young Man picks up the robe. The Sweeper holds out his hands. The Young Man hands the robe reverently to the Sweeper. The Young Man and Young Woman kneel in front of the Sweeper. The Crowd kneels. The Sweeper does not know what to do with the robe. He hands it to the Girl

Sweeper Put it back in the wardrobe, love.

The Girl smiles, accepts the garment, and takes it away

(*Turning to the Young Man and Young Woman*) You're a right pair.

Young Man
Young Woman } We have sinned. }(*Speaking together*)

Sweeper Don't you forget it.

Young Man
Young Woman } We shall remember. }(*Speaking together*)

Sweeper Mind you don't do it again.

Young Man
Young Woman } Never again. }(*Speaking together*)

Sweeper You'll have to drop this king lark, too. You'll live longer and work better without it.

Some of the Crowd remove the thrones

In fact, your family's waiting for you now—two boys and a girl.

The Young Man and Young Woman look up

In a Council flat.

Young Man Overlooking the gasworks.

Young Woman With a view over the railway.

Sweeper You could do worse.

The Young Man and Young Woman stand

Harriet enters breathlessly

I thought you'd been banned for ever.

Harriet The Manager!

Sweeper The Manager? Quick! Help me to clear this lot off the stage.

Young Woman Easy. (*She begins to stamp and clap rhythmically*)

The Crowd looks up, stands up, and joins in. The Young Man and Young Woman start to dance.

Hand joined to hand, everyone dances after them, and off the stage. Everyone exits. At the very end of the line of dancers is the Sweeper, pulling Harriet after him. As they disappear from one side of the stage, The Manager appears on the other side. He looks about, then peers at the Audience. The Sweeper enters, sweeping

Manager What are they doing here?

Sweeper Sitting quietly.

Manager Get them out.

Sweeper I told them to go, but they wouldn't. They seem to be expecting something. I suppose the best way to show there's nothing else is to bow.

Manager Bow?

Sweeper Bow.

The Manager and the Sweeper bow

Harriet enters and takes up a position next to The Manager. She bows

The Sweeper tries to indicate that Harriet should go

While the Sweeper is thus occupied, the Young Man and Young Woman come to the side of the Sweeper and bow

Nonchalantly, the Sweeper starts to sweep across the stage. When he is half-way across, The Manager starts after him

The Sweeper runs off, followed by The Manager. The rest of the Company enter and take a bow. The Sweeper runs back in time to take a final bow with them. Everyone leaves except the Sweeper

The Lights change. The Stage Lights give way to the Working Light and House Lights

So that's what you were waiting for.

The Sweeper props his brush against a corner of the stage and leaves

 END OF PLAY

FURNITURE AND PROPERTY LIST

ACT I

On stage: Nil

Off stage: Brush (Sweeper)
Banners (Heralds)
Whistle (Harriet)
Litter (Harriet)
Pipes, tambourines (Crowd)

ACT II

Off stage: Cup of coffee (Sweeper)
Sandwich (Sweeper)
2 thrones
Crown (Harriet)
Orb (Harriet)
Sceptre (Harriet)
Locket (Lust)
Bank notes (Envy)
Placard: "LOVE, HONOUR, OBEY" (Anger)
Arrows (Messenger)
Rifles (Guards)
Flower (Chief of Police)
Bloodstained white robe

LIGHTING PLOT

Property fittings required: nil
A bare stage. The same scene throughout

ACT I

To open:	House lights on. Working light on stage	
Cue 1	**Sweeper:** "Imagine. Please. Imagine." *Fade house Lights and working Light Bring up spot on* **Sweeper C**	(Page 2)
Cue 2	**Sweeper:** ". . . on Daddy's overdraft." *Bring up general lighting to full*	(Page 10)
Cue 3	**Sweeper:** "Where is that thunderbolt?" *Lightning*	(Page 20)
Cue 4	**Sweeper:** "More. Bigger. Better." *Lightning*	(Page 21)
Cue 5	**Sweeper:** ". . . where I make it strike." *Lightning*	(Page 21)
Cue 6	**Sweeper:** ". . . thunder and lightning?" *Lightning*	(Page 23)
Cue 7	**Sweeper:** "Gone. Right? Go!" *Black-out*	(Page 24)
Cue 8	**Sweeper:** "Lights." *Return to full lighting*	(Page 24)
Cue 9	**Sweeper:** ". . . what an earthquake can do." *Lights flash on and off; steady on at end of storm effect*	(Page 25)
Cue 10	**Sweeper** exits *Working Light up. Stage Lights fade. House Lights up*	(Page 25)

ACT II

To open:	As opening of Act I	
Cue 11	**Sweeper:** ". . . the brain to follow it. Perhaps . . ." *Fade working and house lights. Bring up general lighting to full*	(Page 26)
Cue 12	On general exit after Curtain calls *Stage Lights off. Working and house Lights up*	(Page 52)

EFFECTS PLOT

ACT I

Cue 1   **Sweeper: ". . . on Daddy's overdraft."**   (Page 10)
Distant background music and babble of voices—fade gradually as action proceeds

Cue 2   **Harriet: " . . . banners, bugles, drums."**   (Page 18)
Military music. Stop abruptly when Harriet blows whistle

Cue 3   **Sweeper: "Where is that thunderbolt?"**   (Page 20)
Thunder

Cue 4   **Sweeper: "Good."**   (Page 21)
Thunder

Cue 5   **Sweeper: "More. Bigger. Better."**   (Page 21)
Thunder

Cue 6   **Sweeper: ". . . where I make it strike."**   (Page 21)
Thunder

Cue 7   **Sweeper: "Who's a failure?"**   (Page 21)
Thunder

Cue 8   **Sweeper: "Once more for luck."**   (Page 21)
Thunder

Cue 9   **Sweeper: ". . . thunder and lightning?"**   (Page 23)
Thunder

Cue 10   **Sweeper: "Gone. Right? Go!"**   (Page 24)
Thunder

Cue 11   **Sweeper: ". . . what an earthquake can do."**   (Page 25)
Loud rumble

Cue 12   **Sweeper: "Water-spout."**   (Page 25)
Storm and hurricane sounds build up, then die away

ACT II

Cue 13   **Sweeper: "Oh, come as you are."**   (Page 35)
Fanfare

Cue 14   **Sweeper: "One year later."**   (Page 39)
Baby cries

Cue 15	**Sweeper:** "Two years." *Baby cries*	(Page 39)
Cue 16	**Sweeper:** "Three years later." *Baby cries*	(Page 39)
Cue 17	**Young Man:** "Wait for it." *Fanfare*	(Page 42)
Cue 18	**Sweeper:** "All of you." *Fanfare*	(Page 43)
Cue 19	**Sweeper:** "Pulling the wings off flies." *Drum-roll, suddenly cut off*	(Page 44)

David Campton

2nd may 1924 - 9th September 2006

"he was one of the first british dramahistics to write in the Style of the Theatre of the Absurd"

Attempted to tackle political, technical, sociological, religious views through comedy to lighten the prevading opinions

→ Post world war 2 (late 1950
- existentalism
- human existence has no meani or purpose - communication break down - irrational + illogical speech

↓

Pairing this with tradedy demands firm foundations

The play

- throughout the play characters are introduced, Some invited Some not - David campton Justifies this choice by stating that this characters "have been lurking in the sweeper's Subconscious and therefore eligible for creation"

    ↳ This ideology could bee seen as irong/a mirrored representation of reality as David campton is the sweeper, being God in his own world he has created (the play itself).